FIRE FROM ABOVE

DR. ANTHONY LYNN LILLES

fire

FROM

ABOVE

Christian Contemplation
and Mystical Wisdom

SOPHIA INSTITUTE PRESS
Manchester, New Hampshire

Sophia Institute Press
Box 5284, Manchester, NH 03108
1-800-888-9344

www.SophiaInstitute.com

Sophia Institute Press® is a registered trademark of Sophia Institute.

Library of Congress Cataloging-in-Publication Data

Names: Lilles, Anthony, author.
Title: Fire from above : Christian contemplation and mystical wisdom / Dr.
Anthony Lynn Lilles.
Description: Manchester, New Hampshire : Sophia Institute Press, [2016]
Identifiers: LCCN 2016006733 ISBN 9781622823352 (pbk. : alk. paper)
Subjects: LCSH: Prayer—Catholic Church.
Classification: LCC BV210.3 .L55 2016 DDC 248.3/2—dc23 LC record avail-
able at http://lccn.loc.gov/2016006733

First printing

In memory of
Lucille Dupuis,
Poustinik, Our Lady of Tenderness,
Estes Park, Colorado:
may she rest in peace.

CONTENTS

FOREWORD

In every age the followers of Jesus come to Him and ask, "Lord, teach us to pray."

What we ask for, we receive. Jesus gives us the profound gift of prayer. We knock and the door is opened to us, and we are able to enter into the presence of the living God. We seek and we find the face of our Father, Who gives us our name and calls us to friendship.

Prayer is the promise and a privilege that Jesus makes possible for the children of God. Through Him we can dare to call God "Our Father" and speak with Him in loving dialogue.

Anthony Lilles knows that prayer is the way of life for the Christian, and he has written a unique book. There are many good books that talk about how to pray and why. Lilles aims here for something different. He wants to put out into the depths of the mystery of prayer. He brings us into conversation with the Church's living tradition, drawing from the great spiritual masters and the prayer of saints and martyrs. But Lilles understands that prayer is more than method or technique. Prayer is the life-breath of the soul's relationship with God.

This book causes us to reflect on big questions: What does it mean that we can speak heart-to-heart with the One Who created the heavens and the earth, the stars and the planets? What does the gift of prayer tell us about God, about ourselves, and about the meaning of our lives and history?

St. Irenaeus centuries ago said that the human person fully alive is the glory of God. Prayer is the language of glory, the mother tongue of the human person created in the image of God. In God's plan for humanity, we were made to pray, and through prayer we come to the fullness of who we are meant to be.

Yet prayer, this simple gift of conversation with God, has become a "problem" in our times. As our society becomes more secularized, more hostile to "organized religion," prayer loses its place and purpose.

Our secular culture breeds a restlessness of the spirit. People are busy all the time, living at a constant pace, surrounded by the hum of communications technologies — messages being sent and delivered, contacts being made. There are fewer silent spaces for reflection in our lives, and we are losing awareness that we are created for conversation with our Creator.

We have many options today for spiritualities and lifestyles. But the relationship of prayer is different from that. True prayer always has an "object," a *Person* Whose face we are seeking. Without God, it's as if we are praying with a mirror — we are turned inward, focused on ourselves. Our hearts remain restless, anxious, divided, and not free.

If we are to recover our true humanity in this secular age — the true meaning of our lives as children of God made in His image — then we must return to prayer. A vital dimension of the Church's mission of evangelization is to become a house of prayer and a teacher of prayer. The Church needs to help create the space in our society where the relationship with God can grow.

We need to cultivate hearts that are prayerful and attentive to God's tender mercies and His ways of working in our lives and in the world. Even among believers, prayer can become functional, a chore that we feel guilty if we don't fulfill. So many of us—even those of us in ministries and apostolates—don't make time in our day to pray. We tell ourselves we are too busy, that our work is our prayer. This is a delusion and a temptation that is understandable in our work-driven material society. But we should resist it.

It is true—we can live our lives without prayer and do many good things. But without prayer it will never be possible for us to live as God intends us to live, to accomplish what He wants with the joy and liberty of the children of God. Prayer is not only an instrument for expressing our needs and what we hope to "get" from God. Prayer is our response to God's love, the adventure that begins when we open our heart to the Creator, Who is inviting us to intimacy and communion.

There is a beautiful line in the *Catechism*: "Whether we realize it or not, prayer is the encounter of God's thirst with ours. God thirsts that we may thirst for him" (CCC 2559). We are born with this desire for God written in our hearts. We are not talking about the vague "gods" that we imagine or create for ourselves in our personal spiritualities. We are talking about the true and living God, Who has shown His face to us in Jesus Christ.

Jesus not only makes prayer possible. He is also our model. In assuming our humanity, He shows us the necessity of prayer and what it looks like to pray as a child of God. By His teaching and example, we learn that we can speak heart-to-heart with our Father, Who loves us.

In this book, Lilles reminds us that at times prayer can lead us into a dark night, a desert where the desires of our heart are met with a divine silence that seems like no reply. Yet even the apparent absence of God is His response — a loving call for greater trust, detachment, and openness to His will.

Lilles shows us the deep connections between theology and prayer. That is something else that makes this book unique. It is said that we should do theology on our knees, with prayer. But it is also true that we need good theology to pray. Theology gives us knowledge of God. Prayer brings us to love and serve the God we know.

Ultimately, prayer is about conversion. It is about our growing from the image of God into the likeness of Christ, conforming our lives more and more to the image of our Father's only Son. Through prayer we gaze upon the Lord's glory and, as St. Paul said, we are being transformed into His image, from one degree of glory to another (see 2 Cor. 3:18).

Through prayer we seek to know the will of the Father and to *do* it. And prayer changes worlds—not only the inner world within each of us but also the world around us. Jesus taught us to pray for the Kingdom, and our prayer draws us into all the struggles and injustices that frustrate the coming of His Kingdom. We see the world with the eyes of Christ and become sensitive to the needs and sufferings of our brothers and sisters. Our contemplation of God leads us to commitment and action in history, to share God's mercy and love and to seek to serve His plan.

Prayer is the meaning of our life, and our life is meant to be lived as a prayer—an offering to God, a way of service in love. This is how the Mother of Jesus lived. The Blessed Virgin Mary's whole life was an expression of her prayer: "Let it be to me according to your word" (Luke 1:38).

And my prayer is that through our Blessed Mother's intercession, all those who read this fine book will come to a new awareness of the beautiful privilege that we have to pray—and a new experience of prayer as a dialogue of love that leads us into the merciful heart of our Father.

— Most Reverend José H. Gomez
Archbishop of Los Angeles
April 2016

PREFACE

As the Third Millennium unfolds, the world needs the wisdom that the tradition of Christian prayer offers. Profound societal upheaval extends from the intimacy of marriage out to the most public and international forums. In this particularly difficult moment of history, the faith that we profess as Catholics can be a message of hope. Our faith in Christ Jesus opens up real access to the wisdom of God in a way no other philosophy or religion claims to do. Our faith proposes the way of true communion with one another and with God. It does not offer mere information about God, but an encounter with God Himself through the Risen Lord, who is at work in the world. Yet to avail ourselves of this kind of wisdom, we must take time to seek the Lord's presence and live in intimacy with Him. Without this deeper rediscovery of prayer, the Gospel of Christ remains at the level of a nice ideal. With such a personal rediscovery, a heavenly power is unleashed that can turn the whole world around.

As the current academic dean of Saint John's Seminary in Camarillo, California, and of the Ávila Institute of Spiritual Formation, I believe that a spiritual revolution is unfolding in our times. This present work draws from my first book, *Hidden Mountain, Secret Garden* (Discerning Hearts, 2012). In that work, I proposed that Saint John Paul II inspired this renewal in the course of his many World Youth Days, but especially in World Youth Day '93 in Denver, Colorado. Since that work, however, conversations with students have continued to unfold against new social developments and pastoral concerns.

Today, growing social terror and cultural cynicism coincide with the spiritual revolution initiated by Saint John Paul II. This is not a simple coincidence but instead a sign of divine providence. The Lord desires to reveal His glory in the midst of cultural confusion. He is the light that shines in the darkness, and no political power or principality can diminish His splendor. He has chosen to shine through those who humbly believe in Him, not because they are removed from all the painful ambiguity of the world, but because they live in the midst of this present darkness. Thus, all the wars, religious oppression, and calamities of our times provide a particular occasion for spiritual renewal and the restoration of prayerfulness in the life of the Church.

God desires believers to cooperate with His plan for the salvation of the world. This is a matter of grave importance for the sake of humanity, and He is waiting for us to rise to the occasion. Before all the other many challenges that are part of God's plan in our personal lives, the first undertaking involves a deep reconsideration of our own attitudes toward God, ourselves, those close to us, and our communities.

It is one thing to manage our personal existence by constantly reacting to all the forces that are over us. It is another thing to be lifted above these circumstances and to see them from God's perspective. Here, one discovers a new confidence and resolve, a new freedom and readiness to do what is right. This is what the wisdom of authentic Christian prayer offers.

Not all approaches to contemplation produce this kind of fortitude or certainty. If we are demoralized by the culturally and politically powerful, it is probably the case that we have let ourselves mindlessly accept the precepts of bad religion and spirituality. In every case, bad religion is vulnerable to dehumanizing fanaticism—whether theistic or atheistic. Time spent listening to the Lord, however, can help us rethink some of the thoughtless assumptions that now rob us of the joy Christ means for us to know. A deeper conversation with God can even help us root ourselves in a deeper and richer experience of the life He has given us.

Not all forms of prayer rise to this task. The deepest problems in our lives cannot be psychologized away. Magical thinking, however enchanting it might be, does not offer a coherent word of hope. Lasting salvation is not found before the altars of politics, wealth, pleasure, or personal whims. Prayer and spiritual practices that do not help us find solid ground for the weight of our existence leave us with nothing to stand on when we most need to stand strong and not lose hope. Against spiritual egalitarianism, this book roots itself in the command of Christ and the practice of His Church.

The prayer taught by Christ is based in the truth—the truth about life, about our humanity, about the world, and about God. It is rooted in this truth because it comes from above, where "everything that exists" is clearly seen in the light of God. Although we do not possess the glory of this light, Christ, who reigns over everything, sends us the supernatural life and virtue through which this light shines. When we accept the gift of this prayer from above, its power is unleashed in the reality of this world below and into the reality of our lives here and now.

ACKNOWLEDGMENTS

This work is derived from my *Hidden Mountain, Secret Garden: A Theological Contemplation on Prayer*, originally published by Discerning Hearts, Omaha, Nebraska, in 2012. Thanks to the good theological counsel of Fr. Giles Dimock, O.P., Fr. Raymond Gawronski, S.J., and Fr. Matthew Gutowski, as well as the enthusiasm and hard work of Kris McGregor, the original work surpassed all expectations. In the meantime, many readers of the original work sent helpful feedback that contributed to this new effort. *Fire from Above* would not be possible without the ongoing support and good counsel of David Scott of the Archdiocese of Los Angeles, Dan Burke of the Ávila Institute of Spiritual Formation, and the generosity of Sophia Institute Press. I would also like to acknowledge Matthew Tynan, who has promoted this work around the world and whose friendship was invaluable in completing this present project.

CHRISTIAN PRAYER AND FIRE FROM ABOVE

Humble prayer, here below, brings down fire from above. Whenever anyone places any situation under the shadow of heaven's light with humble sincerity and trust in God, those circumstances can be suddenly ignited in Divine Love. Earthly eyes may not always see this, but the eyes of faith glimpse this splendor. This is the kind of prayer that Christ Jesus commanded His followers to offer. It is the kind of prayer that reveals the glory of God.

As one learns to live by this prayer of faith, the heavenly fire can grow into a profound awareness of the presence of God. This prayerfulness silently contemplates the hidden ways in which He is always at work in the world making all things new. Through this kind of devotion, our humble petitions and thanksgiving converge into wonder and adoration before the excessiveness of His love. And in this contemplative silence, God listens to our concerns and shares His concerns with us—for He treasures each one of us in particular and all of us together and has already implicated Himself in our plight.

This reverent awareness of God's love is known to the Catholic tradition of spirituality as mystical wisdom. Such contemplation is born in an ongoing personal encounter with the Almighty.

The living source of invincible confidence, this kind of mental prayer renews one's whole mindset and transforms one's whole existence — body and soul — into a spiritual offering for the glory of God and the salvation of others. The more one's heart is ablaze with this Living Flame, the brighter and more loving the whole world becomes. Christian prayer is revealed by God as the only sure means to attain this wisdom from heaven.

Seemingly so insignificant in the face of today's political and cultural powers, *true Christian piety* is often treated with casual disregard and even scoffing disdain. In fact, today, persecution of Christians is viewed with unquestioned acceptance and in-difference. Nonetheless, humble faith calls down supernatural power: *fire from above*. The most basic petition, when animated with even the first hint of faith in Christ crucified, lifts *even the most impossible situations* into the warmth and light of God Himself.

Christians call out for this wisdom in the name of Jesus for the sake of their own salvation and the salvation of everyone whom the Lord entrusts to them, even their enemies. They do so with the hope that their prayers will win a prize better than life itself. While those who believe in Christ crucified are soberly aware of their own unworthiness to approach the living God, they also believe that Divine Mercy can overcome their own sinfulness and much more. Thus, they approach prayer as an essential part of their journey of faith.

They follow a pathway that is vulnerable and open to every-thing that the Lord yearns for them to have. If they persevere, they believe that they are always given just what they need in the moment. In this way, every moment becomes the moment that takes them deeper into the mystery of God. Christians are convinced that to make this journey is the very reason that each one of us has been made, and the greatest of believers cleave to this conviction even in the face of death.

A *Testimony to Wisdom from Above*

On a bright sunny day, on a beach in Libya, twenty-one young men in orange jumpsuits were lined up with their backs to the sea. Twenty of these were Coptic Christians from Egypt and Ethiopia. Many had just started their families. Behind each one, a masked guard stood ready. Having been tortured and tormented since their capture, the men were ordered to renounce Christ or face death by the sword.

Each refused. Their simple prayer filled the empty chilled silence. "My Lord, Jesus, my Lord, Jesus," they gently whispered and repeated until the brutal moment when they were shoved to the ground and beheaded.

When the executioners came to the twenty-first man, they knew that Matthew Ayariga was not Egyptian or Ethiopian or even Christian. He was probably from Chad with ties to Ghana. Like the other prisoners, he had come to Libya looking for opportunities to support his family. This was not his fight. Like the other men, however, he was given the very same option, "Do you renounce Christ?"

We do not know all that he was thinking in that moment. We do know that the human spirit resists coercion. We have all experienced how something deep inside rebels against being forced to act against our sovereign freedom. This is especially true in matters of faith and religion. On that February day, he responded with quiet sober resolve: "Their God is my God."

Matthew chose to bind himself to the fate of his Christian brothers by his own blood. This act of solidarity could not have been a decision made without concern for his family. At the same time, his decision of faith defied his tormentors and rebuffed their effort to violate his freedom and dignity.

Two millennia of Christian martyrs help us see the greatness of our religion in the face of everything that threatens humanity. In an otherwise senseless world, their piety offers an unvanquished answer to brutality. This is true not only for those who know their faith in Christ but also for those who do not know it, but trust in the God whom this faith proposes.

The genuine Christian cry for Divine Mercy unleashes power that death itself cannot contain. This kind of piety offers a last bastion for everything that is good, holy, and true about humanity. It grounds itself firmly in the truth that Jesus Christ never abandons those who call on Him, even if they do not yet know Who He is. Instead, the Risen Lord ignites a flame in those who call to Him in faith until they are ablaze with fire from above.

Although God does not desire death or suffering for its own sake, He burns with the desire that goodness and truth be made known. The twenty-one martyrs in Libya are witnesses to Christian prayer. Their effort to pray in extreme circumstances speaks to the nobility of our Faith and the supernatural freedom it provides. Matthew's decision, moreover, was made in the midst of this fire from heaven. I start this work with the witness of these young men so that our exploration of prayer together might benefit from this unfamiliar light and warmth; if what these men witnessed to has stirred your heart, then you have already tasted the fire from above that this present work endeavors to explore.

"I came to cast fire upon the earth; and would that it were already kindled!" (Luke 12:49). Jesus came to cast fire on the earth. Just as the Lord was present to those martyrs, Jesus Christ, burning with love, has come to be present to you at this moment in the most real and personal way. This fire is His love for the

Father and His love for everything the Father has accomplished. Jesus longs for our hearts to be ablaze in its flames.

When we open our hearts to Him, the same wisdom that blazed on that beach in Libya blazes in our hearts too. This wisdom connects us and puts us in solidarity not only with these witnesses but with all the witnesses to Christ who have given testimony and even shed their blood for the last two millennia. As I write these words, I am mindful of those who have been terrorized by public displays of violence, here in America and around the world. When this wisdom burns in our hearts, it also implicates us in their suffering and sorrows—in a communion of mercy.

The Sun of Righteousness (Mal. 4:2) dawns in our hearts, not as a nice wish or a projection of our ego, but as the tender standard in whose glow each life and every action is judged. Not overcome by the cold or darkness of the world, the Risen Lord flashes flames of fire more powerful than any military force or political ideology or social agenda. This Light, however, does not coerce or diminish our intelligence, imagination, intuitions, passions, or freedom. Instead, the Conqueror of Death, who re-veals the truth about who we really are, bathes all this human potential in divine splendor and heavenly tenderness when we immerse ourselves in Christian mental prayer.

This book is about how all that is genuinely wholesome and worthwhile in our personal lives is realized in the mystical wis-dom of the Catholic Faith. In bringing down this fire from above, true beatitude is known on earth, even at the moment of death, by this humble movement of heart. By this contemplation, God reveals us to ourselves, answers our deepest longing, takes away our guilt, saves us from death, and gives us access to a love that is stronger than death. What we are proposing is that this wisdom, at once deifying and humanizing, is fire from above, a heavenly flame that the Lord longs to enkindle anew in our hearts today.

Praying in Search of Wisdom

How is mystical wisdom enkindled in our hearts through prayer? It is a matter of allowing our devotion to the Lord to mature. Contemplation is something every Christian can pursue, and mystical wisdom is essential to spiritual growth. The point is that contemplative prayer and the experiential knowledge it gives are integral to the universal call to holiness.

Even if only a few of us are able to live a contemplative life, every Christian needs the wisdom that comes from mental prayer. Understanding what contemplation is, in fact, encourages us to pray all the more. We need to confront things in our lives that are intrinsically opposed to this effort. Finally, we need to bring spiritual practices into our daily life that will help us welcome the gift of prayer that God has for us. To this end, we have divided our book into three main parts: (1) doctrinal foundations for the pursuit of mystical wisdom, (2) confronting challenges to mental prayer, and (3) the spiritual means for welcoming the gift of contemplation.

We provide the doctrinal foundations of contemplative prayer in chapters 1 through 9. We explore these foundations in relation to the nature of the soul, the indwelling of the Holy Trinity, the mystery of Christ, the Sign of the Cross and sacramental life, and finally sanctifying grace and the theological virtues of faith, hope, and love.

Once we have provided the doctrinal foundations for contemplation, the next part of our work addresses the most difficult obstacles to union with God. Chapters 10 through 12 provide insight into what God is doing in our struggles to forgive and show mercy. In this section we propose that these struggles, when confronted with faith, rather than hindering contemplation, can become opportunities to deepen the wisdom of prayer in the difficult ambiguities of our daily lives.

The final part of our book covers some of the most effective means for growing in prayer. Chapters 13 through 19 highlight how we welcome and protect the gift of contemplation through spiritual exercises, sacred study, and devotion to Mary. Although there are many books that propose various exercises, some of these do not provide good doctrinal foundations, and others seem to suggest that contemplation is an outcome or the result of our own spiritual industry. Our emphasis is on the primacy of grace and our cooperation with what God is doing in our souls. We will look at spiritual practices, including devotion to Mary, as the means by which we give the Lord the space He needs to ignite our hearts with His wisdom.

Throughout this book, in fact, we argue that contemplative prayer has the form of a gift. This gift is from above, a heavenly grace, and thus is not limited by the particular circumstances we face here below or subject to any earthly power. Thus, no matter the circumstances, when we humbly and graciously welcome this blessing from God, it always blesses everything that is good and true about our humanity. Through this kind of prayer, what is in heaven is realized and made present on earth.

Not the attainment of a benchmark proficiency, the fire of this tender piety is a deeply personal blessing given by God to the heart. It is a spiritual gift that makes our devotion to God mature. To welcome this gift requires faith, trust, determination, and perseverance — and yet everything the soul does is no more than a response, an assent, a *fiat* to God's work. This blessing opens to a very tender encounter, a subtle presence "within" of the Trinity of Divine Persons in the unity of one divine nature who love us with a faithful and particular love. We want to propose in these pages that our hearts were made to welcome this gift and that when we possess it, the whole reality of heaven is brought into earthly existence.

Our Approach to Prayer and Wisdom

Against some who see contemplation as an effort to surmount finitudes of being human, we offer a polemic for the gift of God in prayer as intrinsically humanizing. The prayer that He gives is more than therapeutic exercise for good mental hygiene. The wisdom He offers is much more than any technique can achieve. No psychic state or degree of enlightenment or evolution of human consciousness surpasses Him—for He is over all, and, at His right hand, the highest peak of human existence is opened to us.

We propose, in these pages, the very simple and humble movement of faith to God that the Church teaches us to render—a movement that is both unitive and generative. Such contemplation draws us into communion and sends us out on mission in a way that mirrors the Holy Trinity and fulfills the commands of Christ. Only an uncalculated effort, free from worry over "spiritual" results, is open to a wisdom purely focused on what pleases the Lord. This fire from above has the character of mutuality—an intimate sharing between friends that is fruitful and leads to great joy. We are convinced that God is always ready to give just such a gift of wisdom to those who ask.

The contemplative prayer we propose is directed to the presence of God revealed by the Word made flesh. We humbly ask for this gift at the foot of the Cross, the very threshold of the divine nature and the gateway to all that is genuinely human. This kind of prayer is not the mastery of some set of magical practices, but a falling down on one's knees in tears before the One who was crucified by love.

Over and against the latest conventions and popular spiritual fads, this book proposes a humble return to the rich tradition of Christian prayer. This effort to lift up our hearts is a pathway to freedom from a certain heartlessness that has its grip on us. Lifting our eyes from our narcissistic absorption in technology, this contemplative engagement with God and the things of God gives us the liberty to look up and see the wonders unfolding before us. The ultimate escape from a self-absorbed virtual world, this conversation with the Lord reacquaints us with who we really are and reasserts in us the truth for which we were created. Prayer rooted in this vision of truth is pure fire.

It is long past time for those of us who have made baptismal promises to rethink the place of prayer in our lives. We know by faith that humanity, in all its goodness and wonderful possibilities, gravitates toward death. If we simply go along with its broken impulses, we Christians will not only lose our integrity, but we will fail to provide the word of hope that the world waits to hear from us.

As I write this book, dark shadows of terror visit our brothers and sisters — all around the world. Our society and our culture need followers of Christ, especially those of us who are Catholic, to rediscover the mystical wisdom found in prayer. This contemplation is a source of blessing not only for those who receive it in prayer, but also for all those whose lives they touch. This is the wisdom of our twenty-one brothers in Libya whose humble prayer in the face of death brought down into the depths of the world today *fire from above.*

1

FIRE IN THE GARDEN
OF THE LORD

According to Saint John of the Cross, God is the soul's deepest center.[1] He is not suggesting that the soul is spatial or divisible into different parts more or less central to its existence. Nor is he proposing that the soul and God are deep down the same thing. The Carmelite master knows that the soul is spiritual and indivisible, yet created and thus distinct from God. In his poetry, God is relational, a mystery of threefold mutual love out of which all creation flows, including each soul.[2] Created for relation out of the eternal relations of the Trinity, none other than Divine Love is the ground, the deepest center, from which each free, personal "I" draws its life and learns to give itself. The saint is arguing that our whole being finds its rest to the degree that we seek this loving ground and stake our lives on it.

To say that God is the deepest center is like saying that God is the ground of the soul. The soul, in turn, is nothing less than the very garden of God.

---

[1] See Saint John of the Cross, *Spiritual Canticle* 39:14 and *Living Flame of Love* 3:9–10.
[2] See Saint John of the Cross, *Romances: In Principio erat Verbum*, stanza 4.

Not only is humanity meant to draw its life from God, but the Divine Immensity desires to dwell in the confines of our own human frailty. To this end, Divine Love has generously endowed us with inexhaustible blessings. The greatest of these blessings is His personal presence offered to us, the gift of the Holy Spirit, by which we might freely know and love Him in a manner commensurate with the way He loves and knows us.

This means that each man and woman is endowed with great dignity and purpose; we are meant to exist because Love Himself has willed us into being by love, with love, and for no other reason than love. It is through love that the soul is meant to be God's garden. When a soul lovingly receives the gift of the Spirit of love, divine fire dwells in the garden of humanity anew.

Mystical wisdom is a loving awareness of this mysterious presence. The fruit of an ardent search, reverent prayer, all kinds of sacrifices and patience in trials, this wisdom inclines the heart to delight in the Divine Immensity, Who has chosen to dwell humbly within as Guest and Friend. It matures into the realization that God's presence is not only the ground of one's existence, but completely implicated in one's very plight. This wisdom bows in awe over the sheer excessiveness of God's love. It is the font of new desires to welcome and respond to Him in more generous ways—in everything. This mystical knowledge penetrates, not with concepts but with great certitude, that although we can always neglect or even betray Him, Eternal Love has nonetheless created the human being to be a living sanctuary, a paradise where the One who is from above might dwell on earth, a home where He might be freely welcomed for "Who He Is" amid the hostility of the world here below.

The Bible reveals gardens as special places of intimacy and prayer. The garden of Eden, the garden of the burning bush, the garden in the Song of Songs, the garden of Gethsemane, and the garden of the empty tomb can be meditated on as images of the heart. The same drama that once unfolded in those biblical gardens unfolds in the life of every believer. Like the garden of Paradise, this deepest center of a man or woman can be a meeting place with God but also become a place of shame: closed, dark, and cut off. God knew that He risked all kinds of inconstancy, betrayal, denial, and rejection, but He chose the human heart anyway, and this with divine hope.

Is it possible for God to hope? It is true that God does not hope in the same way that we do. In the perfection of His divine nature, God is not subject to the appetite we call hope. On the other hand, if God cannot hope, then it would be impossible for the Word made flesh to hope. Yet, in the prayer on the night before He died, He prays to the Father, expressing His hope in glorifying the Father and sanctifying humanity. Because of the unity of His humanity and divinity, everything He did as man, he did as God. When we consider the order of Persons, we can say that the Son placed his hope in God the Father. This is possible because in God is the perfection of hope. So in this since, God hopes — not for things that He does not know will happen, but infallibly for things that will happen according to the eternal plan of the Father. If we deny this, we deny the theological foundation for the virtue of hope, but we know our hope does not disappoint, and because of this, it must be rooted in a mystery in the very heart of the Holy Trinity. Divine hope refers to this mystery.

God's hope for humanity should confound us and drive us to consider why we exist. This divine confidence summoned us into existence and lives in our hearts with complete foreknowledge of all our failures and inadequacies — and still He calls, undaunted in his purpose and desire. We should draw closer to this glowing mystery; we are meant to know its warmth and light.

To believe that the presence of God abides in the soul means that the intensity of divine glory is somehow able to rest in the wisp of existence that is humanity without destroying its integrity. This garden is so delicate and limited that how exactly it can be filled with the abiding presence of the almighty God and still remain undiminished is not immediately obvious. It is not simply the metaphors that contrast more than compare. We are confronted with a paradox of the Uncreated abiding in what is created, of the unchangeable God establishing Himself in what changes, of the Infinite circumscribing itself in what is finite, of divine power working in human frailty.

When we attend to the One who calls to us with love, we become part of a story and take up our role in a drama that began before the dawn of time and unfolds unto the very end of the ages. In this story, we are not spectators but participants. The soul is a garden, and God's presence a blazing fire (see Deut. 4:24 and Heb. 12:29). This burning bush that we discover on this holy ground within ourselves commands reverence and invites a conversation.[3]

If prayer attends to Him in faith, it can hear when He patiently questions us and even more patiently answers our questions—if only we will accept His mysterious invitation. We discover that He desires to walk with us just as He conversed with Adam and Eve, just as He called Abraham, just as He stood with Moses and Elijah, and just as He traveled with the disciples on the road to Emmaus. Answering this divine desire is the beginning of prayer.

[3] See Gregory of Nyssa, *Life of Moses* 2:19-20.

How is sinful humanity set aglow with divine life and how does divine perfection suffer human misery? We propose with Saint John of the Cross that it has to do with the soul's deepest center. Real relation with God is both the cornerstone and the capstone of the architecture that holds humanity together and allows it to realize its sacred purpose. Because our personal existence is rooted in the Trinity as His image and likeness, there are capacities in the human heart that the Almighty can raise up without diminishing its created uniqueness, but instead perfecting it. His personal presence landscapes the human soul with divine fullness all the while establishing and preserving its integrity. Describing how the soul is a garden of God in the lives of the saints helps us see how Christian mystical wisdom, fire from above, is fundamentally a mysticism of being in relation with God.

The Garden of the Saints

The saints help us examine further the connection between the biblical image of a garden and the heart. They have also considered how God dwells with humanity. The teachings of Saint Anthony of the Desert, Saint Augustine of Hippo, Saint Teresa of Ávila, and Saint John of the Cross all involve gardens. Their stories, in fact, are interconnected and are important for understanding mystical wisdom. More specifically, the story of Saint Anthony greatly influenced the conversion of Saint Augustine, and his conversion in turn influenced that of Teresa of Ávila. Saint Teresa of Ávila in turn formed the soul of Saint John of the Cross. In other words, our tradition connects gardens with the intimacy with God in the soul.

The garden mentioned in the stories and teachings of these saints is not an accidental detail. It has spiritual meaning. The visible points to the invisible. The life we lead in the gardens of this world below needs to be ordered to the invisible, spiritual paradise that is within us. Our ability to offer our visible bodies as a living sacrifice for the glory of God depends on this spiritual renewal of our hearts.

Every man and woman bears a connection with paradise, the primordial garden. Like that garden, the human soul is meant to be a place of order, beauty, peace, and friendship. By considering paradise further, these truths about humanity help us understand the very structure of our nature as capable of communion.

John Paul II points this out in his own teachings on the Theology of Body.[4] In the beginning, man and woman were given to one another as husband and wife in the garden of paradise. In the cool of the evening, in communion with each other, they walked with God in its beauty. That original communion that humanity knew with God involved mutual tenderness, the joy of being together, and openness to new life. Vestiges of this wonder that unfolded primordially and biblically linger in every heart even today.

The heart of each man and woman is like the garden of paradise in this sense: it too is meant to be a place where we encounter God and where we make space for others to walk in our lives and a place where we are tested. Whether or not we realize it, each of us carries the original experience of peace with God and each other deep in our psyche—even though wounded by sin. We long for connection with someone outside of ourselves and with something or Someone above us. In our hearts, we also confront a sense of alienation and disconnection not only from God and others, but even from our very self.

---

[4] See, for example, John Paul II, *Man and Woman He Created Them: A Theology of Body*, trans. Michael Waldstein (Boston: Pauline Books and Media, 2006), 161–169.

To help us understand this interior experience, the Church proposes that the wounds of Adam and Eve's original sin and the consequences of our own sins weigh down our hearts and create distance between us and others and between us and God. If we are ill at ease with our own existence in the world, this is because, as an icon of paradise, the deepest center of our humanity has also been lost by sin. Paradise and paradise lost are both part of primordial and biblical human mystery.

Left to our own human resources, we do not have the means on our own to reestablish the connection that has been lost. There is enmity in our most sacred relationships. Meaningfulness in our lives is subject to futility. Our industry and fertility are subject to corruption and death. We are assailed by all kinds of weakness, inadequacy, anxiety, and voids. Every human heart is threatened by this same doom, even as it continues to yearn for the connections for which it was made and strives for the fruitfulness it was created to know. Since all our natural potential exists under the weight of these difficult circumstances, we need help over and above our limited power and created nature. Only assistance not subject to these earthly contingencies can allow us to realize the truth of our existence. This heavenly help God longs to give us through loving union with Him.

The unity of humanity and divinity in love that Christian prayer realizes is salvific. Faith in Christ mysteriously reconnects our hearts with the original human experience so that what is impossible for us on our own becomes possible through Him. Only the prayer of faith can bring divine wisdom to bear on our need for connection and on the burden of guilt that weighs on us and on the reality of death with which we are confronted.

Christian contemplation is about seeking the One who is from above to help reestablish the paradise that we were meant to know here and now. We can find Him because He has come down into this world below in search of us. He does not offer us merely the paradise that Adam and Eve once knew—*not paradise lost*—but a more wonderful garden, in which God is present in ways that not even Adam and Eve could know. This garden is an established part of a new heaven and a new earth, not as a distant future reality, but as a reality breaking in, "begun and still in progress."[5]

Saint Antony of Egypt

Sometime after his conversion and dedication to live a disciplined life of prayer, Saint Antony of the Desert began to desire greater solitude. So many visitors were coming that he was not able to spend time in silence with the Lord. He was glad to provide hospitality to those who came to ask him questions, but he also knew that the wisdom that God was giving Him in prayer was even more important. He began to make plans to go deeper into the desert.

In the midst of this project, the Lord questioned Antony. It is a powerful thing to allow God to question us in prayer and to permit Him to show us the secret motives of our heart. As Antony explained his plans, the Lord warned him that if he continued with his own designs, he would not get the results that he was looking for but instead the exact opposite.

This kind of prayer that is open to a deeper discernment of God's will is very important for those who desire a more perfect life of prayer. When we are vulnerable to the Lord, sharing our innermost secrets with Him, we are able to benefit from God's counsel. He who gave us the desires of our hearts has a way to

---

[5] See Blessed Elizabeth of the Trinity, *Heaven in Faith*, no. 1 and *Last Retreat*, no. 1.

fulfill them, but He waits for us to ask and allow Him to share His plan. In the case of Saint Antony, the Lord asked him for his trust. The Lord wanted to lead him to the inner mountain, Himself.

Letting go of his own designs and what was familiar to him, Antony chose to follow the promptings of the Lord into unfamiliar places. This required a deeper kind of trust and confidence from him. Because the saint chose to trust the Lord over his own designs, God was able to lead him to a secret place, a hidden mountain. When he finally discovered the place that God had prepared for him, Antony was filled with a deeper joy and peace than he had ever known before.

The hidden mountain that Saint Antony was permitted to find is a symbol of those sacred places—not only geographical, but above all spiritual—to which only the Lord can lead us. We are not clever enough to find them ourselves. They are hidden in places too unfamiliar and uncomfortable for us to think of on our own. But the Lord works in unexpected surprises—if we will only trust Him. It is in this place that Saint Antony finally finds the freedom to pray. He builds a cell and a beautiful garden and enjoys a tender friendship with the Lord.

Like the secret mountain, the garden is also a symbol of an interior reality. The garden speaks to the joy and simplicity of a life of prayer. Saint Antony's soul is at peace in the presence of God, and God abides in peace with him.

The ancient contemplative ideal was that the grace of Christ restored humanity to the original friendship with God enjoyed before the Fall. The Fathers of the Church called this the Adamic life. It meant that humanity's original justice and innocence was realized anew through a life of contemplative prayer and discipline. Those who lived the discipline of the Christian life were walking with God in paradise once again.

There is, however, a great difference between the original paradise and this new paradise. In the old paradise, we were untested and not vigilant. We enter the new paradise only to the degree that we are tested and learn to be vigilant. Our crucified Master leads us there when we follow in His footsteps.

Saint Augustine of Hippo

Starting in the middle of the fourth century, a number of Roman citizens were exposed to the writings of Saint Athanasius, some of which describe the life and teaching of St. Antony. Uninspired by a culture that was becoming increasingly indulgent and turned in on itself, they were stirred by Saint Antony's freedom to leave everything for the service of God. The secret of his freedom was a life-changing encounter with Christ. Somehow, merely hearing about Saint Antony's experience caused others to encounter Christ as well.

This was the case for Saint Augustine. In book 8 of his *Confessions* he discloses how the Lord rescued him from the darkness of sin and gave him the light of confidence to live the Gospel. Like Saint Antony, he would find his peace through a conversation with the Lord in a garden.

Augustine wanted what Christianity had to offer. On a practical level, however, he deemed it impossible. He had lived a sexually active life outside of marriage for quite some time. How could he be chaste for Christ when he was held back by so much lust and fornication?

Yet, that is exactly what he found after having read *The Life of Antony* by St. Athanasius. In this work, Saint Augustine discovered, as did his contemporaries, that the Christian faith offered a fullness of life that nothing else in the world could provide. Those who put their trust in the Lord acquired an interior strength and wisdom to do things that were over and above the personal limits imposed by sin, custom, and convention.

Long before he was led to the hidden mountain, Antony learned the power of listening to the Lord and allowing Him to question and to give us counsel. After having lost his parents as a teenager, Saint Antony was anxious about managing the family farm and taking care of his sister. He himself had long desired to dedicate his life to prayer and the service of the Lord. One day, after praying about this very concern, he arrived at Mass just in time for the Gospel reading, and he heard the story of the rich young man proclaimed.

In this story, the young man wants to know how to inherit eternal life, and after questioning him, Jesus looks at him with love and tells him to sell everything he has, to give to the poor so that he will have treasure in heaven, and then to follow Him. Saint Antony discovered the Lord's look of love when he heard this passage. It was as if the Lord were speaking directly to him in a personal way. He found new freedom in those divine words and sold his possessions, entrusted his sister to some elderly widows, and embraced a life of prayer.

Augustine marveled when he learned this story. The Lord spoke to an uneducated man directly, and this man recognized and responded to His invitation. Augustine also wanted to give up everything and radically follow the Lord. He was especially attracted to the Christian purity and chaste lives that Christians lived. He even wanted to embrace total continence.

Unlike Saint Antony who was worried about family matters, Augustine's problem was sex. He was afraid that if he chose to follow the Lord, he would not be able to handle it. Could he really live without the joys of sexual pleasure?

This vexed him. On the one hand, he could no longer stand the thought of continuing to live as he had. He knew he needed something more. On the other hand, he did not see how this was possible based on his own resources and natural gifts. The inner pain and torment were leading him to understand that only the Lord could provide such a grace, and the only way to get this blessing was to humble himself and ask.

It is at this point that he ran to a garden to be alone and begged the Lord in tears. It is not accidental that Augustine tells us about this garden in Milan. Gardens are special places of encounters with the Lord—not only Eden but also the holy ground of Moses' burning bush or the garden in front of the empty tomb where Mary Magdalene met the Lord.

In Augustine's garden, he would learn a great secret that would free him, allow him to live with himself, and allow him to embrace conversion of life. In the intimacy of a garden, he poured out his heart to the Lord, begging for the grace to make a new beginning, and, like Antony before him, he heard a voice commanding him to read the Bible. When he obeyed the voice, he felt as though the Lord spoke to him directly through the words of the Bible in the same way Saint Antony did. Only the words he read were from Romans 13:14: "Make no provision for the flesh."

Like Saint Antony, the effect of this encounter with Jesus through a biblical passage was immediate. Saint Augustine says that the light of God's confidence flooded his soul. The darkness and the doubt were no more. He clung to the Word of the Lord, Whom the words of Sacred Scripture had revealed.

Saint John of the Cross

Over a thousand years later, the conversions of Antony and Augustine influenced Saint John of the Cross, particularly his understanding of the soul as a garden for the presence of God. Like Saint Antony, Saint John of the Cross connects the spiritual life with a journey that leads to a garden. As with Saint Augustine, the garden is a place of a new beginning. Yet in the writings of Saint John of the Cross, an actual physical garden is not part of his conversion—at least so far as we know. Instead, he employs the rich imagery of a garden to describe a place of encounter where God and man might meet. For him, the garden is a spiritual, interior reality, the center of the substance of the soul.

Saint John of the Cross was an important part of the renewal of mystical wisdom in the Church. Through his relationship with the founder of the Carmelite Reform, Saint Teresa of Ávila, he provided solid spiritual counsel and vision for this return to contemplation. While he does not speak about the direct influence of Antony and Augustine in his own thought and experience, Saint Teresa does. The rich imagery of the garden that is part of these testimonies imprints itself in her spiritual doctrine. She goes to the garden of Gethsemane with the power of her imagination in prayer, and she describes the soul as a garden that needs to be prepared for the Bridegroom, who wishes to rest there. She would have used this same imagery to discuss the nature of her prayer with Saint John of the Cross both in communicating her ideas about the Carmelite Reform and when she went to him for spiritual direction.

Saint John of the Cross devoted his life to supporting Saint Teresa's work, because, like her, he knew how important mystical wisdom is for the life of the Church and how it requires a disciplined life of faith. He would have appreciated that, like Antony and Augustine, her doctrine also proposes a connection between a garden, God's presence, and the soul. But in her thought this connection is by way of spiritual metaphor. Just as she uses the image of the garden to help us understand the relationship of God's presence to the soul, Saint John of the Cross takes up this connection in his own writings and prayer.

Like Saint Teresa, his own experience of the garden of prayer would not happen in a physical garden. Instead, his writings explore a spiritual garden that he learned to visit by faith and contemplative prayer. At the same time, he embellishes this spiritual imagery by bringing to bear his own interpretation of the Song of Songs. In this biblical love poem, the garden is described as a place of intimate encounter, mutual self-disclosure, and fruitful union. By means of this imagery, he proposes that in order to enter into fruitful union with God, we must search for Him by faith in the garden of our hearts, where He is hidden. These insights into the soul as a spiritual garden did not come easy. Instead, they were the fruit of contemplative prayer offered in the face of brutal treatment, humiliation, and patient perseverance.

While he was serving as a spiritual director at the Monastery of the Incarnation, a group of fellow priests and religious broke into his cell, kidnapped him, and put him in prison. This would be the beginning of a long ordeal during which thoughts about the garden of the soul would become an important consolation.

John's captors believed that they were acting with due authority to bring to obedience this obstinate little priest who was fanatical about prayer and austerity. They tormented and tortured him to get him to change his mind. They promised him all kinds of comforts if he would only renounce the Carmelite Reform that Saint Teresa had initiated. He refused.

The Carmelite Reform that these fellow religious were trying to crush was about a renewal of mental prayer. They were opposing (even if unwittingly) deeper intimacy with Christ in contemplation and a more disciplined way of life to protect this kind of prayer. Saint John's conscience was bound not to renounce practices that he knew pleased the Lord. He also understood that his ministry and way of life was duly authorized by the Church.

On the other hand, the authority and the practices of his persecutors were ambiguous. It was not clear to him that he should renounce the contemplative life or his solidarity with those who also bound themselves to the reform of contemplative prayer that Saint Teresa had started. Instead of capitulating to coercion and manipulation, he accepted being misunderstood and despised. Locked in a closet under a stairwell with no light, save only a slit high above his head for a little fresh air, he was left in squalor to fast on bread and water for nine months.

Whereas Saint Antony dealt with the need for a deeper trust in God in the face of possessions and Saint Augustine dealt with chastity in the face of lust, Saint John of the Cross struggled with obedience in the face of ambiguous lines of authority. It was in pondering the soul as a garden of the Lord's presence that helped him grow in mystical wisdom even under these conditions. He rooted this contemplation in the Song of Songs, which he had memorized. Now, whenever he had the strength to return to prayer, he was able to draw from the rich biblical truths the inspired text proposed to him.

By meditating on this book of the Bible, Saint John of the Cross was feeding his prayer with thoughts that have helped sustain the greatest mystics and reform movements in the Church. The mosaics of the ancient Church and the writings of patristic authorities suggest that the Song of Songs was carefully prayed over by generations of faithful. Like the great contemplatives before him, Saint John of the Cross found in its verses a source of hope, and this is especially so in the way this book guided him to think about the nature of the soul and God's presence in it.

The fruits of his contemplation are captured in his poem *Spiritual Canticle*, in which he describes the soul as a garden with imagery from the Song of Songs. His commentary on his poem applies this description to particular challenges and moments of grace that one confronts in the spiritual life. These are the challenges and the consolations waiting for every soul that will journey within to seek God's presence. This journey of faith ignites the heart with longing and leads to a personal encounter that establishes one's whole being in peace and joy—not for the absence of trials but in the very face of them.

In this protected trysting place, the Lover and the Beloved are heroes who overcome the many challenges that threaten their friendship, engagement, and marriage.[6] The way Saint John of the Cross describes it, the garden is a protected space for love because the Bridegroom has made his beloved strong against all her enemies. The imagery he takes from marriage in the world below is a sign of this heavenly marriage above. If earthly marriage is under the banner of love, even more so is the marriage of Christ and the Church and the bond between Christ and the soul.

Christ is the Bridegroom who has called us into this garden and clearly initiates the drama of developing intimacy and intensity of love. He is the principal actor, but He counts on our readiness to seek, to recognize, and to respond to Him. Thus, we are not passive observers or spectators, but full participants in the drama of this friendship unfolding in the depths of the soul. We are participants not only as unique individuals whose particular

---

[6] See Song of Songs 4:16–5:1.

spiritual journeys delight Him in unrepeatable ways, but also as beings who are in communion with one another in the life of the Church. In Saint John of the Cross, the real drama of life unfolds in the depths of the heart, not only for the individual believer but for the whole mystery of the Church herself.[7]

There are some important observations to make on the basis of the Carmelite Doctor's insight. First, Christian mysticism is relational because the mysteries of the Church and the soul in which this wisdom is realized, enjoyed, and made fruitful are themselves principally relational mysteries. That is, they are bridal realities nuptially ordered for indissoluble union, faithfulness and mutual fruitfulness with God. Like a bride who is ready to give herself to her bridegroom and tenderly receive the gift of his very life, the Church and the soul are mysteries created to be the Bride of Christ. In the Church this reality has already begun to be realized. In the soul, this mutuality is pledged at baptism and anticipated in the Eucharist, but not fully realized until the life of faith matures.

This brings us to a second insight. Not only is Christian mystical wisdom a relational reality, but it also has a progressive character. The more this kind of prayer unfolds, the more intense its mutuality with God becomes.

When faith matures, the soul, like the Church, is not only a garden in which the personal presence of God rests, but it is also the Bride to whom He yearns to give Himself completely. The mystical wisdom of contemplative prayer raises desires of

---

[7] Saint John of the Cross poetically develops the nature of this drama in *Romances, In Principio erat Verbum*, stanzas 3–4 and connects the life of the soul and the Church in *Spiritual Canticle* 30:6–7.

faith that are actually commensurate with these desires of the heart of God.

Saint John of the Cross is fully aware of the progressive nature of this wisdom. He describes this wisdom as a ladder by which we ascend into heaven as we descend into humility.[8] The more humble the soul, the more God is attracted to it—just as the humility of the Church draws God's presence in ever new ways. The more God is drawn to the soul, the more the soul wants to respond with generous receptivity to His goodness and excessive love.

This leads us to a third insight. The progressive nature of this wisdom toward greater and more intense mutuality also has an ecclesial dimension. Not only is the soul like the Church in this way, but the mystery of the Church is connected to each soul, the more that soul grows in wisdom. The soul and the Church are fashioned to respond to this dynamism in solidarity, and whenever this response is given, soul in the Church and Church in the soul realize their highest calling and become the praise of God's glory. Just as a bride lives no longer for herself but for her Beloved, the Church does not exist for herself but for Christ and for the salvation of the world. Likewise, the soul does not exist as an alienated entity that must close itself off in acts of self-preservation but has been created to give itself for God and for those whom God entrusts to it—and this is realized through its communion with the Church.

Finally, the relationality of contemplative wisdom in the Christian tradition not only progresses to greater communion with God and the Church, but it is also spiritually fruitful for the world. A careful study of the ladder of mystical wisdom described by Saint John of the Cross in book 2 of his *Dark Night*

---

[8] See Saint John of the Cross, *Dark Night of the Soul* 2:18.

of the Soul suggests this. But for our purposes, our exploration of the soul as a garden needs to make the connection between relationality and fruitfulness more explicit as it brings into relief its nuptial character.

The generative dimension of this relational mysticism involves the Bride's devotion to the glory of the Bridegroom, and the Bridegroom's devotion to His Bride. In the life of the Church, this fruitfulness is sacramentally and liturgically celebrated in the waters of baptism. In the mystery of the Christian life, this fruitfulness is realized through the Corporal and Spiritual Works of Mercy. This means unless a soul becomes more merciful through its practice of prayer, it must be vigilant about whether its prayer is completely open and vulnerable to the coming of the Bridegroom who yearns for His Bride to bear abundant fruit.

Authentic contemplative prayer is where this spousal devotion of the soul and God and of the Christ and the Church finds its deepest expression. This mysticism for which the heart is fashioned is nothing less than an exchange of gifts between the Bridegroom and the Bride, a sharing of the gift of one's very self with the other. This exchange of gifts is superabundant and generates a deep dug fountain of blessings and graces for the salvation of the world.

The Dwelling Place of God

God has fashioned our very being as His dwelling place, a place where He wants His presence to abide as loved and known. To this end, He established us so that He Himself is our deepest center. Wherever God is present, there is always sacred order, wholeness, due proportion, and radiant clarity even when no one else knows and sees it but Him alone. He wills, however, that we do see something of this great work by faith. He wants our cooperation as He recreates the inner spiritual space animating each man and woman. This free personal soul—a reality so much more than a mere state of consciousness, no matter how enlightened—has been chosen by God as His preferred and desired habitation, and He waits for our help to accomplish this wondrous work. We, however, are not always familiar with the ways in which He makes all things new. He is at work in ways we do not understand and do not find convenient: ordering, purifying, restoring, expanding this dwelling place so that He might find His rest in our love and knowledge of Him.

Contemplative prayer, the surrender of our minds in attentive receptivity to the Lord, gives God space to do this work. This kind of wisdom is a matter of choosing to live by love even when we do not feel or understand love, choosing to pray in love even when love seems completely absent. This mystical knowledge is a matter of faith that confidently affirms what it does not see clearly but believes out of devotion to the One who has called it.

It is on this point that Saint John of the Cross pleads with his readers to spend their prayer seeking the presence of the Lord within—in this garden of God. Just as Jesus declares that "the kingdom of God is within" (cf. Luke 17:21) and Saint Paul asserts, "You are the temple of the Holy Spirit" (cf. 1 Cor. 6:19), John of the Cross passionately affirms, "O soul, more beautiful than all other creatures, you are so anxious to find out where your Beloved abides. You want to look for Him and to be united to Him. Know that you yourself are His home, His secret chamber, and His hiding place."[9]

---

[9] Saint John of the Cross, *Spiritual Canticle* 1:7, in *Collected Works of St. John of the Cross*, trans. Kieran Kavanaugh and Otilio Rodriguez (Washington, D.C.: ICS, 1991), 480.

God contemplates the human creature, although such a small part of His handiwork, as His garden par excellence. What He contemplates always comes into being. The more the heart welcomes Him into its weakness and inadequacy, the more His richness and strength are able to dwell in it—purifying, enlarging, and transforming its dimensions. He delights that the more humble this garden, the more many opposites may coincide in it: the material and spiritual, the visible and invisible, what is above and what is below, the heavens and the earth. What makes men and women most beautiful is this unfathomable capacity to be so raised on high that they can come to bear the constant transforming impact of God's limitlessness on their limitedness and, in so doing, find the sheer joy of becoming more fully human and more wholly alive.

2

THE HOLY TRINITY:
FURNACE OF LOVE

In our last chapter, we began to explore the wonder of the soul as the dwelling place of God. In this chapter, we reflect on how the Trinity is the dwelling place for the soul, humanity's true home. This has happened by means of divine decision, a sacred personal choice for humanity, made deep within the heart of God and revealed to us by Christ Jesus. To this end, the night before his death, the Word of the Father offered His supreme prayer that He might be in us as He is in the Father: "Father, I desire that they also, whom thou hast given me, may be with me where I am, to behold my glory which thou hast given me" (John 17:24).

This infallible petition of the Word made flesh is completely rooted in the analogy He asserts between "I in them" and "You in me." The mystery of God and the divine election of humanity indicate the relational character of Christian mysticism. A reciprocal coinherence is at work: if the deepest center of the soul—that is, the place where the soul finds its rest—is the loving presence of God Himself creating it *ex nihilo* (out of nothing), this divine ground to the soul's free personal existence has gratuitously decided to be the dwelling place for humanity in a personally present and particularly concrete way.

Why is God drawn to make His home in us, and why does He want us to find our home in Him? God is drawn by love — whether it is the love that He has already ignited in us or the love that He yearns to ignite. The Trinity, Three in One and One in Three, is the secret and compassionate dynamism that holds together everything that is genuinely human. Every man and woman is made to be ablaze with this eternal circulation of freedom, truth and life — fiery icons of God's existence, of His goodness, and of His holiness in the cold darkness of the world.

While some hold God to be a static, impersonal, and indifferent absolute, the Christian faith lays claim to a dynamic, personal, and fully present Divinity. He is too great for any category of thought to contain Him, yet the dynamism of His one nature evokes a response, and the mutual love and knowledge of the Divine Persons summons creatures into existence ex nihilo to bathe them in the sheer wonder and goodness of "what is."

Humanity is meant to mirror this fullness, to be caught up in this dawning refulgence and to manifest this divine glory in the world. The Father sent His Son into the world that we might know this most sacred truth, not only with our minds, but, even more, with our whole being, body and soul. To behold the revelation of this excessive love by Christ through a simple act of faith in prayer is to be vulnerable to the whole human vocation, its greatness, and its ultimate destiny. This is exactly the mystery to which Christian mystical wisdom attends and in which it is rooted.

Great mystics and saints describe God's presence as fire.[10] Like the fire of the burning bush, this flame of eternal love, by

---

[10] This is biblical; see Hebrews 12:29. I have in mind Saint Gregory of Nyssa, *Life of Moses* 2:19–20 and Saint Augustine, *City of God* XX:12:13.

virtue of its own nature, does not diminish distinctions, whether created or uncreated. It maintains and reveals, and does not collapse, that analogy of being and faith by which men humbly recognize that they are not God.

Unlike an impersonal absolute that collapses everything into its system, this holy fire always ignites all manner of differences between things and people anew in life-giving wonder, for divine being, love, and truth are never diminished and never diminish anything that is good, noble, and true.[11] Instead this divine power is manifest only in the inexhaustible multitude of things in the world. Whether angels or men, creatures become more fully the creatures they were made to be, the greater the warmth and light of God in them. For similar reasons, Saint Irenaeus taught that the contemplation of God is the very life of humanity.[12]

The uniqueness of this Christian vision of God is often underappreciated in discussions of prayer. Some seek salvation in *something* that they believe is above it all: an idea or a system, a cause or an agenda, a feeling or a fantasy, psychological or social, spiritual, or material. Worship is rendered on these altars of achievement and insobriety with the conviction that attaining material or spiritual power over one's life requires only the right amount of human industry and cleverness, or else the right drug. Such forces, whether they are worshipped as divine or simply as projections of one's psyche, are not what Christians know as the living God.

Those who pursue these other gods are burdened by the pain of not being connected to anyone or anything, at least not in any meaningful or lasting way. These idols do not, in the end,

---

[11] See Saint Gregory of Nyssa, *Life of Moses* 2:25.
[12] See Saint Irenaeus, *Against Heresies* 4:20:7.

provide a meaningful answer to our deepest unfulfilled desires, nor the dis-ease we have with ourselves, nor the doom of alienation and eventual dis-integration of our personal existence that hangs over our lives. Instead, this kind of religion diminishes our dignity until we are completely defined by the things we produce.

Exotic techniques and complex religious systems may promise a pathway out of this futility, but these are nonetheless vulnerable to the greed, ego, and unmet psychological needs of whoever has proposed them. Behind the latest marketing schemes of the next new spiritual program for self-improvement is just another soul or group of souls subject to the same ambitions and futility as the rest of us. Even if we escape the delusion and intoxication of this religious commercialism, an abyss of cynicism and nihilism looms on the other side.

True. Measurable outcomes, spiritual enlightenment and religious breakthroughs may enchant for a time. In the end, these all fail to satisfy the longing for connection, forgiveness, and hope that rages within our being. Only fire from above—the warmth and light that come from the Father, the Son, and the Holy Spirit—can do that.

Not an Outcome, but a Gift

Whether they base their practices in modern science, esoteric philosophies, or magical thinking, those who practice non-Christian forms of prayer often expect to attain satisfying and measurable outcomes. Whether they do so for the sake of personal or communal enlightenment, or a shared sense of relief found in good mental hygiene or to find a euphoric escape from the terrors and burdens of life, they want a result that can be measured and repeated in terms of its therapeutic or social benefit. Some even claim to be advancing the very evolution of new forms of human consciousness that they believe is part of the development of our species. In any event, they grasp for a result.

In such impersonal forms of wisdom, categories of mutual recognition and confidence do not apply. Instead, distinctions and differences are eventually to be left behind. One's own contingency and particularity is absorbed or dissolved into the universal and abstract—as if life in our created world were not a gift but a burden from which to be freed.

Christian mysticism, nonetheless, proposes a completely different answer to life's burdens and spiritual growth—not an *outcome to be grasped for* but instead a *gift to be received.*

Christian mystical wisdom is about receptivity and vulnerability to heaven's warmth and light, realities that no earthly industry can produce. A gift from above, this wisdom surpasses all earthly attempts to grasp for an Absolute. More than a limited means to earthly outcomes in life here below, this wisdom *from above* orders and lifts everything in this world now to the hidden glory that lies ahead.

The gift that is Christian mystical wisdom is no less than a personal encounter with the One who comes from above. Rather than an escape from humanity and the human condition, the deeper the union with God found in this wisdom, the more fully and particularly humanizing this wisdom becomes. This kind of contemplation grows in vulnerability and readiness to welcome the Trinity, in whose image and likeness man is made to live. The more open it is to the vision of God in faith, the more lively one's humanity becomes.

The Trinity—Hidden Source of the Prayer of Faith
Christian contemplation is prayer in the name of the Father, the Son, and the Holy Spirit. The very mystery of God involves

eternal relations, and this is why each human being, in the image and likeness of God, also needs to be connected to others. What is more, the divine personal encounters (that is, the divine relations) that subsist within the very life of the Trinity are the basis for all analogous encounters with the Trinity in this world below. Thus, the wisdom of Christian prayer is a relational participation in God's mystery. This kind of mysticism subsists in the most tender human connection, and within a whole communion of these human connections, with the Almighty.

All of this is to propose and argue that the highest truth for Christian contemplation is the Holy Trinity. Everything else that the vast horizon of this wisdom takes in is subordinate to this uncreated primal and ultimate mystery. Christian prayer implicates one in a mystery of eternal connections and divine dynamism that delicately and subtly humanize the heart, so that in this prayer, one becomes more fully himself. Through contemplation of God, that is, through vulnerability in a listening and receptive silence to the personal distinctions and mutual relations of the Father, Son, and Holy Spirit as subsisting in one nature, one is established in the communion and integrity that come from God. One also comes face-to-face with one's personal vocation and mission in this furnace of divine dynamism: Three Persons in one nature, not static but at once life begetting, begotten, breathing forth, and breathed in, and this with awesome fullness and splendor. To attend to this divine heartbeat is to allow the divine command to be fruitful, to be merciful, to be perfect, to follow, and to love to echo into the very core of one's whole being.

The Holy Trinity unfolds a wonderful plan, a defining adventure for those who will welcome this mystery with silent readiness of heart. The Father, Son, and Holy Spirit bring forth into existence everything and everyone in a superabundance of gentle solicitude and patient concern for great purpose. No one's life is accidental; each one is particularly treasured and loved, an irreplaceable part of His great story, a wonderful story that tells the heart-piercing glory of God. This story of the Trinity at the heart of Christian mystical wisdom has the form of a thanksgiving. An offering of joyful thanks for the glory of the Father by the Son in the unity of the Holy Spirit, this exchange of love in the heart of God is the very source from which proceeds every blessing here below and in the heavens above. Christian contemplation beholds this Eucharistic sacrifice in the heart of God and in this vision is baptized in a meaningfulness and fullness of life that this world cannot contain but yearns to know.

The Eternal Eucharist

Contemplative prayer in the Catholic tradition is, as we say of the Eucharist, "right and just." This kind of contemplation takes its decidedly Eucharistic form from the life of the Trinity. This kind of contemplation is right and just because the very mystery of God is rooted in an exchange of blessings in which the fullness of justice and fittingness reside. Just as the Trinity is not static and disinterested but is an eternal exchange of divine knowledge, love, and joy, so Christian prayer is also a thanksgiving, an exchange of blessings between God and man. Christ crucified, who has entered into the heavenly sanctuary with His risen humanity, has established this connection in his very person. Through the gift of the Holy Spirit, Whom He has merited to send us, His prayer before the Father resides in us and animates our prayer. Christian contemplation in fact shares in the exchange of love between Father and Son in the Holy Spirit in the order of grace.

This kind of contemplation claims bold access to the Ultimate Reality that brings humanity and the cosmos itself into existence. It dares to seek and obtain the greatest of blessings, not on the basis of its own merits, but because of what Christ accomplished on the Cross. The wisdom of Christian prayer does so for the glory of God and the salvation of the world.

There is a Eucharistic mystery in the heart of God. It is known only by its reflection in faith through the prayer of Jesus disclosed in the Scriptures and continued in the Church. This great primal thanksgiving is such an unfathomable and surpassing mystery, all description and explanation falls short. Yet the splendor and glory of this eternal movement in the bosom of the Trinity completely permeates the mystical wisdom of the saints and is expressed in the Mass.

Christian prayer, especially in both its contemplative and liturgical expressions, unfolds under the shadow of the Trinity's hidden glory. In the Mass, rituals conveying mutual recognition, blessing, and freedom express a movement of heart from God to man and from man to God. This prayer realizes by God's grace the reconciliation of the heavens and the earth, of time and eternity, of saints and sinners, and all this in a loving communion too great for the present moment to contain. Yet this is only an image, albeit a true and effective image, of an even greater reality in the inner life of God. Contemplative prayer suffers this immense mystery and excessive love as it is disclosed to the heart by faith, and in hushed adoration, tastes the Trinity's splendor.

The origin of this kind of prayer is the Father. With a completely perfect paternal affection and awareness, He has always begotten, He beheld, and He blessed His Son. Moreover, He is pleased in His Son and desires that His pleasure be known and shared with others.

The Father's jubilation is shared with the Son. According to Saint John of the Cross, the Son evokes paternal ecstasy—a going forth from self—because the Father sees in His Son the fullness of His own goodness. The Son likewise rejoices in the Father and offers everything back to Him. This shared plurality and unity in Father's goodness completely delights both Father and Son together.[13]

This sheds light on the sense of mutuality and solidarity signified in the Mass and sought in contemplation. Joy is love that possesses what it desires. Jubilation is a joy that cannot contain itself but needs to be expressed. In begetting the Son, the Father possesses in Him unfathomable and infinite goodness. He cannot contain His joy over the One He has begotten. A joy that must be expressed proceeds from Him so that in recognition and thanksgiving over who the Son is, Father entrusts everything to the Son, and this evokes the Son's thanksgiving.

The Son likewise rejoices in the Father and entrusts everything back to Him in the same eternal act of jubilant thanksgiving. This uncontained joy and thanksgiving that mutually *proceeds* from the Father and the Son constitutes a subsistent relation in God's nature, a Divine Person: the Holy Spirit. Everything that the Father entrusts to the Son is entrusted in the Spirit, and everything that the Son gives back to the Father is given back in the Spirit. The Mass and contemplative prayer are informed by this same divinely shared jubilation: the Father, Son, and Holy Spirit eternally recognizing and entrusting the inexhaustible goodness of the divine nature in one another.

One way the Mass participates in God's eternal jubilation is when the priest places the offering on the altar and blesses it at the preparation of the gifts. Here, the liturgy signifies the action

[13] See Saint John of the Cross, *Romance: In Principio erat Verbum*.

of Christ, who accepts our gifts to offer them on our behalf to the Father. Just as the Father expresses His jubilation by entrusting the Son with everything, we also rejoice to entrust everything to the Father through Him. The delight of the Father is expressed when He sends the Holy Spirit to sanctify our gifts and entrust us with what is most beloved to Him as Father: the Real Presence of His Son. In this way, the joy of the Church participates in the delight of the Father and the Son.

Flowing from the liturgical prayer, contemplation can participate in this same divine mutual jubilation until God's very life mysteriously imprints itself in the heart and lifts up Christian existence. Like the Mass, this mystical wisdom is thus oriented to awe, wonder, and joy over the presence of God, His total and unexpected otherness that is at the same time astonishingly close and accessible. Just as the origin of all is rooted in blessing and recognition of the Other through an act of love, so too the Mass, so too mystical wisdom.

Yet the Mass does not exhaust this wisdom. After all liturgical prayers have concluded and the rites have drawn to a close, this awareness of God's presence mysteriously unfolds in the heart. This kind of silent knowledge before the Lord feeds on the joy and confidence that the Father and the Son themselves share. This sacred stillness of heart opens to a discovery of self that one acquires only by giving oneself away to God in love.

The gift of self that mystical wisdom inclines us to make is also rooted in the very life of the Trinity. Having received everything from Father in great love, the Son blesses the Father in return with thanksgiving. His offering of thanks brings to bear everything that He has received in a perfect act of love. When the Word became flesh, this act of love was revealed through His death on the Cross.

The more contemplative prayer searches this mystery of Christ, the more the soul desires to offer itself to God. The soul desires and is actually able to make this sacrifice of self not because of what it accomplishes in prayer, but because of what the Holy Spirit is accomplishing in it.

The shared breath of Father and the Son, proceeding from the Father and the Son, the Holy Spirit is gift — the One given and received, unchanged but always new. He searches the deep things of God and comes to testify, to convince, to lead us to all truth. To welcome this Uncreated Wisdom is to be plunged in the mystery of Christ and to be raised with Him. Through pure grace, the Holy Spirit freely communicates to the soul that humbly welcomes Him what He has received in the depths of God: the blessing of the Father and the thanksgiving of the Son in a transforming harmony of love and knowledge.

This divine mystery of eternal thanksgiving, this mystery of the Trinity, eagerly yearns to abide in the human heart through the gift of the Holy Spirit. Since the Holy Spirit is in the Father and the Son, and the Son and the Father in the Holy Spirit, when we welcome the Holy Spirit in our hearts, the whole Trinity dwells in us. For those who embrace the life of faith, the heart becomes a place where the eternal thanksgiving of God resounds and where we learn to give thanks with Him.

Hospitality to God in Prayer

To be plunged into the unity of the Three Divine Persons in one divine nature is a gift to be carefully welcomed and reverently adored. When we rise to this kind of prayer, the presence of the Trinity sets our humanity fully aglow — the whole range of our earthly existence can be set ablaze but never be destroyed in these flames. We are made to be completely seized by this tender mutual communion of the Divine Persons in one undivided nature.

In the freedom of the Divine Persons, we are meant to find our freedom by grace. In the plurality of divine subsistent relations that constitute this uncreated unity, the secret of the created human person is revealed. It is a mystery of mutual, tender, selfless love.

Humanity is the living icon of this love revealed for creation, in creation. This is a vocation not to an abstract perfection but to a concrete and particular perfection in the order of creation. We cannot realize this ourselves but only by divine help. Not by escaping or avoiding, but by accepting our lives as a gift, we discover the secret of God's hidden providence at work in all the ambiguities of our existence. It is a matter of rendering thanks for what we know by faith. We possess this divine secret not to the degree that we surmount the limits of our created nature or succumb to impulses beneath its dignity, but only insofar as we become what we were made to be.

We become what we worship. As religious beings, we submit our existence to that to which we render sacrifice. Many believe only in the gods of their own making and will only worship the work of their own hands. But to worship what our hands have made is simply to worship ourselves—whether at the altar of career, money, reputation, control, or self-indulgence. All of this is too shallow for the human vocation. Self-worship is always dehumanizing. We can give our hearts only to forces opposed to our humanity when we do not give them to the One in whose image and likeness we were made.

The presence of the Trinity abiding in our hearts in a personal way is a great mystery that saves us from alienation, guilt, and the power of death. Through making the eternal communication and freedom of God's own life vulnerable to our existence, the Trinity has endowed us with new meaning and has opened up a new way to deal with the challenges of life. Through this gift of divine life, we discover the gift of living life to the full and receive everything we need to answer the noble calling of our humanity.

This means that the deepest truth about being a human being is that we are known and loved by God, not in a general, vague way, but in a profoundly personal manner. Just as the divine nature is above and beyond human nature, so is the particular love the Divine Persons have for each one of us and all of us together an excessive love beyond all measure, exceeding every expectation. The Trinity chooses to be with us in our plight—the common plight we share and the particular plight each of us faces. The Almighty has taken up our cause both as individuals and as a web of friends and family bound together with strangers and enemies. The living God is on our side, each one, everyone—awaiting us with love. This is why He has come to be with us.

The gift of His presence reveals to each of us, as His very image and likeness, our highest calling. The human person is most himself when, in hushed adoration before the heart-piercing mystery of the Trinity, he allows himself to be bathed in the sheer wonder of God's personal presence within his heart and on that holy ground sanctions an offering of his whole existence to God as a gift in return. In fact, only by giving this gift of self to God and to those whom He entrusts to us do we discover this truth about ourselves—the truth of our being in the image and likeness of the Trinity. The perfection of this mutually willed communion, a solidarity freely chosen by God and man, is the ultimate reason that God summoned us into being and called us to Himself. The future of all of humanity—its relation to itself and the whole world — is completely characterized by this relational mysticism.

We are essentially embodied spiritual creatures, religious beings brought forth in love and for no reason other than love. All our failures and shortcomings are secondary to this. In fact, God is constantly using our weaknesses and limits to accomplish His plan in us — as if this were the preferred mode of divine providence.

Christ's prayer in us through the indwelling of the Holy Spirit proceeds not by forcefulness or aggression. It does not seek to surmount human weakness or annihilate our inadequacies. Instead, it is content with the humble acceptance of our frailty. This prayer of the Lord unfolding in us boasts in the trials and difficulties it suffers for love of God. Our prayer, especially when it is silenced in adoration and confidence before this mystery gives the Lord the sacred space He needs to share His gentle and patient strength with us.

When we make this wholly simple movement of love in prayer, no matter how tentative or frail or inadequate our effort, we make room in this life for the fire of Divine Love. We exercise this humble trust by accepting our hearts for what they are and trusting that God's love is greater than our failures. We make this simple movement by silencing the rancor and obsessions that attempt to overthrow our loving attentiveness. Spiritual reading, the Rosary, and the Chaplet of Divine Mercy can help to this end. But these are simple means to help rouse our devotion and attend to God. In the end, we must allow the Holy Trinity to draw us into the silent but unconquered dynamism of Divine Love, truth, and freedom. In this way, eternal love can burn in our hearts and set our mortal bodies aflame. And to have the whole of humanity ablaze with this truth, this love, this life — this is the goal of God's coming to abide in us.

3

ELIZABETH OF THE TRINITY

In the last chapter, we presented the indwelling of the Trinity as a vital doctrine for those who want to grow in mystical wisdom. We would be mistaken to assume that the personal presence of God in our hearts that this doctrine proposes is anything less than the chief mystery of Christian prayer. At the same time, throughout the centuries this truth has often been misunderstood and neglected by many in the Church. In many ways, the renewal of contemplative prayer in the life of the Church has tended to coincide with a rediscovery of this important truth. A prophet who helped the Church rediscover the importance of this teaching for our time is Blessed Elizabeth of the Trinity.

Born as Elizabeth Catez, she would spend hours "searching" for the Lord in her heart. In the hiddenness of faith, she experienced God's presence as a source not only of rapture but also of strength. There was an excessive quality to God's love that drew her into silence.

The catechesis at the time was preoccupied with the renunciation of sin and the requirements of God's justice. The French government had enacted an aggressive policy of secularization, and many in the Church were anxious to uphold traditional piety and morality. Rather than affirm the mercy of God and His indwelling presence, preachers and catechists emphasized the need to struggle against sin and avoid the punishment of Hell.

Blessed Elizabeth never contradicted this teaching, but it did not help her understand her experience in faith. Nonetheless, she took the teaching seriously. It helped her live a converted life and make some helpful resolutions. At the same time, the disjuncture between what was being taught and what she was experiencing in prayer puzzled her.

As a teenager, she found that the writings of Teresa of Ávila contained language that helped her express some of what she was experiencing. She also began to talk to people of prayer who opened up new avenues of sacred doctrine that were more helpful to her. When she turned twenty-one, she entered Carmel.

She is most known for a prayer that she wrote shortly after her profession: "O My God, Trinity whom I Adore." Part of this prayer is quoted in the *Catechism of the Catholic Church*.[14] In fact, Blessed Elizabeth is the only twentieth-century mystic quoted in the *Catechism*.

In the passage where her prayer is cited, the *Catechism* proposes that the ultimate end of God's work is the perfect unity of creatures with the Holy Trinity. Moreover, this ultimate purpose for the whole cosmos is not to be realized in some distant future. Instead, the *Catechism* explains, the unity that God desires to have with us can be anticipated now, in the present moment, because we are to be the Trinity's dwelling place. It is to illustrate this point that part of Blessed Elizabeth's prayer is cited, including her words, "Make my soul your heaven, your beloved dwelling and the place of your rest" (CCC 260).

---

[14] In fact, she is the only twentieth-century mystic quoted in the *Catechism*.

This teaching marks an important development in the history of contemplative prayer. Up until the end of the nineteenth century, the Church had largely neglected the importance of the indwelling of the Holy Trinity in the Christian. This is part of the reason for the catechesis that Blessed Elizabeth received. Preachers and catechists simply were not attending to this doctrine.

Concurrent with this deficiency in teaching about the Trinity was a deficiency in teaching about the importance of mental prayer in the life of the faithful. Some advocated that in fact there were two kinds of holiness: an extraordinary holiness achieved through esoteric feats for the contemplative elites of the Church and an ordinary holiness realized through simple vocal prayer for the rest of the faithful. This dangerous dichotomy caused some to see themselves as above and beyond the ordinary communion of the faithful and the ordinary holiness of the Christian life.

A Pope who taught at the time of Blessed Elizabeth would begin to shake up some of these assumptions. In his encyclical *Divinum Illud Munus* Pope Leo XIII asked the Church to rediscover the gift of the Holy Spirit and the indwelling of the Trinity. As he approached the final years of his pontificate, he had come to the conviction that a greater awareness of the Holy Spirit and the many gifts He brings would deepen the spiritual life of the Church.[15]

Blessed Elizabeth of the Trinity was one of the first beneficiaries of this new direction. Devotion to the Holy Spirit and an awareness of the indwelling of the Holy Trinity in the soul are important aspects of her writings. The influence of her work helped many contemplatives receive the new direction Pope Leo was recommending.

[15] See Pope Leo XIII, *Divinum Illud Munus* 1, 10.

Many contemplatives have shared how helpful her writings were for them, particularly the prayer quoted in the *Catechism*. Even the most austere religious communities have found solid food for contemplation in her writings. They speak about the importance of a deeper devotion to the Divine Persons of the Trinity as one matures in contemplation and claim that Blessed Elizabeth's writings and her prayer have helped them in this more than any other modern source of spiritual doctrine.

Vatican II's Dogmatic Constitution of the Church orients the Church to the universal call to holiness.[16] While there are many forms and expressions of the Christian life, we are all called to the same holiness.[17] This is because by baptism, we have already received the gift of the Holy Spirit and through this gift, the Trinity dwells within our souls. We are meant to know and love God through this powerful presence. The presence, in fact, draws us into our hearts and into the deepest truths of our existence. This means that although there may be many ways to pray, mental prayer or contemplative prayer ordered to Christian holiness is something that all the baptized can practice.[18]

In her prayer, Blessed Elizabeth connects God's presence in heaven and His presence in her soul. Heaven is not a simply a future reality, but a reality breaking into the present. She understood the indwelling of the Trinity as a presence establishing her in peace. God's presence meant the beginning of heavenly way of life that anticipated the life that was to come. In her thought, God's presence is the deepest center of our soul and at the same time an inexhaustible abyss.

---

[16] See *Lumen Gentium* (LG) 40.
[17] See LG 41.
[18] Cf. LG 42 and CCC 2710.

The pathway to this heavenly life proposed by Blessed Elizabeth is one of prayerful recollection. That is, she would habitually collect herself, her intellect, her emotions, and her imagination into silence before the presence of the Lord within.[19] She did this with the hope that He would establish her in a great stillness. This meant renouncing and resisting passing fantasies and vacillating whims that opposed the will of God. It also meant prayerfully placing the joy of her soul in those things that she found humiliating and difficult.[20] She held that this kind of prayerful pathway was a descent into a kind of double abyss: the abyss of her own nothingness and into the abyss of God's mercy.[21]

She does not view the abyss of our own misery as coexisting with the abyss of Divine Mercy, nor does she hold that our personal existence is simply absorbed into a divine absolute. Instead she speaks of an "impact" and an "encounter." When we encounter this immensity of God's presence in us, when it impacts our soul, we are not the same. We become interiorly harmonious, the praise of God's glory.[22]

Elizabeth learned this kind of prayer as a child as she sought to take on her own fiery temper. She viewed self-possession and self-control as an important life project. She discovered prayer as an indispensable means to this end.

Although she was very loving and very devoted to prayer from an early age, gentleness did not come easy for her. She felt movements of anger that sometimes threatened her most important

---

[19] See her retreat written for her married sister, *Heaven in Faith*, no. 3.

[20] See ibid., no. 8.

[21] See ibid., no. 4.

[22] See ibid., no. 43.

relationships with family and friends. For Blessed Elizabeth, as for many who want to serve the Lord, this form of interior misery often expressed itself in an explosive lack of gentleness.

Rather than run away from her weakness, she came to see her struggles as opportunities to rely on God in a deeper way. Her moments of struggle, rather than distracting her from God, put her in touch with the misery she suffered deep in her heart and thus became occasions for deeper prayer and more profound recollection. Elizabeth's writings are filled with a beautiful wisdom that one learns only by suffering the truth about how God works. Conversion to Christ does not make our misery magically go away. In Blessed Elizabeth's writings, one's misery is the pathway to Christ.[23]

You Are a Temple of the Holy Spirit

Blessed Elizabeth built up the Church through bringing the sacred doctrine of the divine indwelling to bear in contemplative prayer. Her writings help believers enter deeper into silent prayer because she developed a doctrinal understanding of the Trinity commensurate with the way God disclosed Himself to her. Yet, for her to arrive at this harmony of doctrine and contemplative prayer, the disjuncture between the catechesis and contemplation that she experienced as a child needed to be addressed. Blessed Elizabeth might have ignored or downplayed the perplexity that deeper prayer brought to her understanding of the Faith. Instead, she confronted it by seeking the counsel of other contemplatives and theologians. This opened up many important moments of grace for her.

---

[23] See her retreat that she wrote for her sister, a married woman with young children, *Heaven in Faith*, 4.

A Dominican witnessed to one moment of grace where prayer and doctrine came together for her. He met Blessed Elizabeth before she became a nun at the Carmelite monastery in Dijon. When she explained her confusion, Père Irénée Vallée instantly understood the catechetical ambiguity and how this robbed her of a deeper confidence in prayer. Instead of downplaying sacred doctrine, he reasserted better teaching as the basis of her contemplation. Quoting Saint Paul, he explained to Elizabeth: "Do you not know that you are a temple of the Holy Spirit?" (cf. 1 Cor. 6:19).

Blessed Elizabeth's experience of the Lord was validated in an instant. These first few words opened her to an even-deeper intimacy with the Lord. Enraptured, she no longer heard the exact explanation. Instead, she was wholly attentive to the Word to whom they pointed. While her prayer took her completely out of herself and wholly into God's presence, the priest continued to explain the meaning of the indwelling of the Trinity. In the wisdom of Saint Thomas Aquinas, in which he was steeped, he explained how the indwelling of the Trinity begins at baptism and increases the more open we are to the grace of God.[24]

The Holy Trinity dwells in our hearts to be loved and adored by grace. Grace is a participation in the life of the Trinity that flows through the Cross of Christ into the depths of our being. Producing all kinds of beautiful thoughts and desires, this new life allows God to give Himself to us so that we can enjoy His presence more and more.

A holy thought that moves us to love makes our mind like Christ, and the stirring of holy affections that move us to love and devotion renders our heart like the Holy Spirit. When our

[24] See Saint Thomas Aquinas, *Summa Theologica* I, Q. 43.

mind is more Christlike, He gives Himself to be possessed in a new way by a deeper faith. When our affectivity is more imbued with the movements of the Holy Spirit, the fire of God consumes us in love.

Because God is ineffable, the greater our likeness to the Son and the Spirit in these ways, the more the indwelling presence of the Holy Trinity extends and deepens. Our greater and greater likeness to the Trinity draws the Divine Persons in ever new ways, surpassing all expectation and joy. From this standpoint, it is normal that we should receive constant new presences of Christ in the power of the Holy Spirit in new ways as our life of prayer matures.

The wisdom of Saint Thomas on this point rests on a great truth about love. Love establishes likeness; and the greater the likeness, the greater the love. When our souls become more like God by every increase of grace, we grow in freedom to love and know Him in a deeper way. He also comes to help us because, when the indwelling of the Trinity increases through the spiritual missions of the Son and the Spirit, it is always for some great purpose — some part of God's plan He has chosen to fulfill through us.

The Indwelling: Contemplation

Blessed Elizabeth never heard a word of this explanation. The Dominican relates that as he continued his explanation, she was completely lost in prayer. One word of truth became an occasion of contemplation for her. In this case, the answer she needed was Saint Paul's question: "Do you not know that you are a temple of the Holy Spirit?"

This question turned her heart to the truth that was borne on the words of the Bible. The Word of the Father speaks into our real situation, even when we have mistaken judgments or have had poor catechesis. Sometimes, it is not the explanation but instead the simple proposal of what we actually believe.

The power of what the Church proposes is a matter not only of its intrinsic veracity but, even more, of the coherence of Church teaching with the profound gift that God wants to communicate. God desires to give Himself completely, and the teaching of the Church is ordered to this divine desire. In this case, Saint Paul's question proposes who we are in the face of the new kind of divine presence that the Trinity desires for us to know.

Whenever we are put in touch with our identity before God and the desire of God, this moment of actual grace can become a profound moment of prayer. What a given doctrine actually explains and the desire of the Trinity for perfect unity can suddenly coincide in a moment of union. This union is very fruitful, not only for the individual who receives it, but also for the whole Church, which somehow benefits from this outpouring of mystical wisdom.

Père Vallée witnessed Blessed Elizabeth succumb to a profound moment of prayer, a kind of ecstasy in which, although her body was physically present, she was entirely caught up in the things of heaven. Scholars who are familiar with the life of Blessed Elizabeth note that this moment prayer of rapture was not a rare experience for her. Other friends noticed that she seemed to be caught up in prayer at times. Every time such a grace is given, it is decisive and fruitful because the fire from above is always transforming in generative and unitive ways.

This particular grace in the life of Blessed Elizabeth, although one among many, testifies to the connection between sacred truth about the divine indwelling and the wisdom arrived at in contemplative prayer. One aids the other even if the precise explanation of doctrine is secondary to the actual supernatural reality the doctrine proposes. The purpose of any doctrinal explanation is ultimately the communication of this reality of the Trinity that is beyond words. Yet, in good doctrine, the words are commensurate to the gift of God's presence and help order the mind to it. The doctrine of the indwelling of the Trinity disposed Blessed Elizabeth to a prayerful union with God.

This particular doctrine is essential for a Christian understanding of mystical wisdom. We have seen that this is a relational mysticism with a bridal character. It is meant to be unitive and generative. Blessed Elizabeth would continue to try to understand the contemplative prayer unfolding in her heart. The Carmelite Doctors would help her receive these truths in a deeper way, and the more she received these truths, the more her experience of the indwelling in prayer would increase.

In particular, Blessed Elizabeth came to see God as a "Consuming Fire" and a "Furnace of Love."[25] Saint John of the Cross influenced her toward this. For him, the presence of the Trinity in the soul is like a living flame of love, catching our whole being on fire.[26] The great Carmelite Reformer believed that God is the soul's deepest center[27] and that one thought filled with Him is more valuable than all the rest of creation combined.[28] Thus, the Carmelite Doctor directs us to enter into our hearts with faith and seek the Lord, Who is hidden the depths of our being.[29] Blessed Elizabeth also emphasized the presence of the Trinity in

---

[25] See *Heaven in Faith*, nos. 13 and 14.

[26] See Saint John of the Cross, *Living Flame* 1:3, 14, 17.

[27] See ibid., 1:12.

[28] See Saint John of the Cross, *Spiritual Canticle* 1:6 and *Sayings of Light and Love* 32.

[29] See *Spiritual Canticle* 1:10.

all its immensity in the soul.[30] For her a simple contemplative gaze at this mystery is the entryway into our true home.[31] This simple movement of love in the heart toward His presence allows the Lord to communicate His radiance and make the soul the praise of glory.[32]

[30] See *Last Retreat*, no. 44.
[31] See *Heaven in Faith*, no. 1.
[32] See *Last Retreat*, no. 8.

4

THE ENERGY OF
CHRISTIAN PRAYER

Christian prayer is rooted in the truth that Christ crucified is fully God and fully man. The prayer of the Lord is *theandric* — the highest expression of the perfect unity of divine and human energy in His Divine Person.[33] *Theandric* comes from the Greek words for God (*Theos*) and for man (*anthropos*). To say that the Lord's Prayer is theandric means that when Jesus prays, although He is God, God prays as man, and although He is man, man prays as God. This is why the Father always hears His prayer and why His prayer raises the hearts of men. In Jesus, God hears humanity's prayer because humanity has learned to cry with a divine voice. In Him, all humanity hears God because God has learned to cry with a human voice. The supreme moment of this theandric prayer was expressed on the Cross. All Christian prayer comes from and goes to this last wordless cry of prayer offered by the Word made flesh.

When the Father sent the Son into our tired old world, the Father was giving humanity to His Son *in this whole new way*. In assuming humanity as a particular man, the Son now opens up the ability to pray and give thanks to God to each individual

---

[33] See Saint Maximus the Confessor, *Ambigua* 5.

man and woman *in a whole new way*. When the Son of God prays as the Son of Mary, He puts into human speech and devotion the inexhaustible exchange of blessing and thanksgiving to which He gives substantial expression in His Person. Whenever anyone offers prayers in the name of Christ, he joins himself to this divine and human reality.

Perfect praise and thanksgiving offered in the unity of this saving mystery is the beginning and final purpose of the Christian life.[34] For those who believe what the Word of the Father revealed, God has implicated Himself in the plight of humanity in the most intimate way, assuming our frail nature and filling it with His own power and life. In the Lord's own particular human soul, the presence of God dwells in perfect fullness and in His Divine Nature, and at the same time human souls in all their particularity and uniqueness are given an eternal place to abide together in the order of grace through faith in Him. This perfect unity of humanity and divinity attains its fullest achievement in His Divine Person — the Eternal Son of the Father who is the ultimate source and summit of all unity of man and God.

By the grace of divine adoption, Christians analogously participate in this eternal relationship and extend what Christ expresses in His own humanity through the life and prayer of the Church. They are adopted into this divine Sonship so that Christ's manhood and strength informs their prayers too — while at the same time, animated by His perfect humanity, the fullness of His divinity is given them.

The Risen Lord in fact prays in them by their bold faith in Him. Their prayer becomes the revelation of His prayer extended

---

[34] See *Sacrosanctum concilium* 10; LG 11.

into space and time, here and now. Christian prayer is therefore essentially a relational reality, a personal encounter between God and man, made possible by the eternal Son of the Father and the Son of Mary.

Risen and continually sent into our hearts by the Father in the power of the Holy Spirit, the Son reveals the mystery and discipline of prayer. In the Bible, His prayer is so attractive that His disciples beg Him to teach them to pray like Him. His prayer itself teaches how to pray (CCC 2607).

The Witness of Saint Thérèse

Saint Thérèse of Lisieux, Doctor of the Church, not only deeply understood the Lord's desires and expectations for us but also felt this grace and shared it with others:

> He thirsts for love. Ah, I feel it more than ever—Jesus is suffering thirst. He only meets ingratitude and indifference over and over among the followers of the world. Among his own he finds (*This is so overwhelming!*) so few surrendering themselves to him without reserve, understanding the tenderness of his love.[35]

Saint Thérèse sees the thirst of Christ as something painful and difficult to bear. In other words, this thirst is not appropriated as a vague metaphor for a simply sentimental idea accidentally to our faith in Christ. Instead, it is an existential, essential, and heartrending reality that we confront in our relationship with Him.

[35] See Thérèse's letter 196, written to Sister Marie of the Sacred Heart around September 13, 1896, trying to provide her with an explanation for her approach to the spiritual life.

She distinguishes the followers of the world from the followers of Jesus. She expresses no astonishment that those who follow the discipline of the world should not welcome Christ. They have no idea Who He is and why He has come to them. She asserts, nonetheless, that their ingratitude contributes the thirst that He suffers. In other words, rejection, even by those who do not know Him, disappoints Him.

Saint Thérèse is not overwhelmed by this state of affairs. It simply is the reality Christ confronts in the world. What overwhelms her instead is what she observes about those who do follow the Lord. Christ's thirst is made all the worse because His own followers do not surrender themselves to Him without reserve. This desire in the heart of Jesus was not simply a *fact* to which Saint Thérèse wistfully assented. It was a theological reality — meaning a deeply grace-filled human reality that impacted her prayer. How this is possible is explained, at least in part, by what our tradition calls the grace of divine adoption.

The Prayer of Christ in Us

When we join Christ by faith, the Holy Spirit moves us with the thoughts and affections of the Word made flesh. Our subjectivity is not our own but is caught up in a more beautiful mystery. The Holy Spirit brings our wills into conformity with the Lord's will. Through the Holy Spirit praying in us, what we pray bears relation by faith to Christ's prayer. In this movement of love and communion, Christ's prayer and ours remain distinct but not separate. The Holy Spirit brings our hearts into harmony with our great High Priest.

This means our unique petitions, in all their particularity, in the concrete circumstances from which they arise, are each endowed with inestimable value. As we articulate the deep longings of our hearts and entrust them to God, the Lord hears them according to the communion that we have with Him.

It is beautiful to think about the analogy between Christ's prayer and ours that this suggests. This mystery of His prayer did not cease at His death. All the ways He expressed His devotion to the Father is given to us through the mystery of our faith.

If, as a child of Nazareth, Jesus makes pilgrimage to the Temple, Christian prayer is also in the form of a pilgrimage to the Father's house.

If His prayer echoes in the hidden quiet of ancient Nazareth, Christian prayer must echo behind the closed doors of our bedrooms and in the heart of our homes.

If He prays the psalms by heart daily — bowing in the morning, raising His hands like incense in the evening, and musing on His heavenly Father through the night, we must allow the affections of our hearts to be formed by the Bible and the Liturgy of the Church.

We find Him ardently in conversation with his Father through the night in deserted places, mountains, and gardens. Christians who are serious about the life of prayer also frequently withdraw for this same conversation. They take up these same struggles and strive to offer this same devotion to the Father.

The Pattern and Power of Christ's Prayer

The pattern of the prayer of Christ is not merely an external example of how to pray, but actually forms the very nature of Christian prayer. After His baptism, He goes into the wilderness and devotes Himself to supplication, fasting, and resisting all forms of dehumanizing irrationality that threaten the human heart. What is begun there continues throughout His ministry. And it continues in our lives after our baptisms.

Jesus rejoices when He recognizes His Father's work. He raises His eyes to heaven. He calls out with joy. He blesses God and offers thanksgiving at meals, even when it appears that there is not enough to eat or when He knows that He will be betrayed.

So powerful is His prayer that He makes the blind see, the deaf hear, the lame walk, the leprous whole, the demonically oppressed free, the dead come back to life, and the sinner forgiven. He weeps over death in prayer. His prayer frees His friends from death.

He prays sweating blood over the plight of those who would reject Him. He dies asking that even His enemies be forgiven. At the same time, the Lord teaches His disciples that they will do even greater things in His Name.

Jesus' devotion to the Father was so dynamic, so beautiful, so compelling that the disciples begged Him to show them how to pray. Yet when the Lord taught his disciples to pray, the only technique He promoted was petition and thanksgiving rooted in unshakeable confidence and vulnerability before our heavenly Father. The disposition of the heart and the virtues that come from Christ characterize, more than any method, how Christians are to pray.

The Way the Lord Commanded Us to Pray

By tradition, Jesus is believed to have given His great teachings on prayer on the Mount of Olives, not far from the garden of Gethsemane, at a place now commemorated by the Church of the Pater Noster. The ancient Byzantines believed Jesus ascended into heaven in the same vicinity. This hill stands between Jerusalem and Bethany, between where His enemies and His friends lived. The events recalled in this sacred geography symbolize the nature and place of all Christian prayer: listening to the Word and responding to Him, in the midst of one's friends and enemies, for their sakes, on our journey to the Father's House.

The teachings of Jesus concerning prayer are straightforward and sober. He lists petitions that ought to be prayed for, describes the interior attitudes one should adopt in prayer, and warns against using prayer to manipulate God or impress men. Although He directs his disciples to seek the Father in private solitude, He also promotes praying with others and promises to be with those who gather in His Name.

By prayer, He establishes a New Covenant that He seals with His own body and blood. This New Testament is the source and summit of all Christian prayer.

His supreme wish before the Father is that His followers might dwell in unity with Him and one another in the Father. He takes this wish all the way to the death He freely accepted for love's sake, and by so doing shows us the painful secret of love, the grace of subordinating our will to God's will. Real prayer has the form of love, and we cannot love except at our own expense.

His last wordless cry on the Cross echoes in all genuine prayer. This cry is the life breath of God flowing into the dying hearts of men and women to raise them up. At the same time, Christ's dying breath is a perfect offering to the Father of all that is humanly good and beautiful. Because its source is ever in Him, Christian prayer has the power of love unto the end, a love that cannot be conquered by death.

At the right hand of the Father, the eternal prayer of the risen High Priest is forever acceptable to God. The Father is eternally pleased in the prayer of His Son. This kind of prayer is not limited by time or space because it flows from the unending source of time and space. It is no longer subject to suffering, even if it suffers for a while the rejection of an indifferent humanity.

Indeed, such suffering is now subject to the Victor over death. Although this Judge of Heaven and Earth delays for the sake of His mercy, the Day of Justice is ever close at hand.

How We Have Access to the Prayer of Christ

This experience of the mysteries of the Lord, with all their apocalyptic force, is not remote from the practicing Christian. The Holy Spirit communicates this prayer deep in the heart through a gift of grace called the divine indwelling. It is the ever newly present prayer of Christ in the Spirit dwelling in the deepest center of the baptized that causes Christians to pray anew in the Spirit. The bodies of the baptized are true temples of the Holy Spirit—God dwells with us in the fullness of our being, making sacred even our bodies.

Besides the indwelling, there is another way the prayer of Christ is present as a living reality in the Christian life: Body and Blood, Soul and Divinity—His Real Presence in the Blessed Sacrament. Under the veils of bread and wine, the power of Christ's prayer issues forth into the hearts of those who partake of this mystical banquet and even flows into those who behold the Eucharist with faith. By this Real Presence, He truly takes into His heart all our deepest needs, makes them sacred in the very blood and water that flowed from His side, and offers them to the Father.

His Eucharistic Presence, by its very nature, is never static, but always dynamic. It is the true center around which the whole cosmos revolves. In perpetual thanksgiving, intercession, and adoration of the Father, the dynamism of Christ's prayer by which He comes to us also draws us to Him. The loving gaze He bestows on us through the Blessed Sacrament leads us to gaze upon Him in return, even when His presence is completely hidden by brutality and suffering in our lives.

Those who discover this gaze know even in the midst of un-imaginable catastrophe that He comes in power and glory. The very foundations of the world may be shaken, but rooted in Him they stand firm. Heaven and earth will pass away, but the Word made flesh will remain forever.

5

DE SIGNACULO
SANCTAE CRUCIS

Since ancient times, Christians have begun to pray by blessing themselves with the Sign of the Cross. No one really knows how old this sign actually is. By A.D. 204, Tertullian, a Father of the Western theological tradition, was already referring to "*signaculo sanctae crucis*" as ancient practice.[36] This blessing roots our prayer in our redemption, our baptism, our Faith, our Church, and our Lord Himself.[37]

The Church entrusts this sign to catechumens as they prepare to enter the waters of baptism. It is a physical, bodily expression of prayer rooted in the bloody work of redemption Christ offered with His own body. Christian prayer is not a disembodied endeavor: it has a physical dimension to it because the Christian faith is an embodied faith—a faith in spiritual truth that must be expressed in our very flesh and blood.

---

[36] In defending a Christian soldier persecuted for refusing to wear the military garland, Tertullian discusses these traditional Christian practices. See *De Corona Militis*.

[37] Jean Daniélou discusses its origins as related to baptism in *The Bible and the Liturgy*, 1st ed. (Notre Dame, IN: University of Notre Dame Press, 2002).

Once he enters the waters of baptism, the Christian's body is made a member of the Lord's body. His very life is no longer his own, and his body is no longer to be used for sin. Instead, although he will often fall short, everything he does is to be for the glory of God.

In this spirit, Tertullian describes this sign as a regular part of Christian life at every step along the way, whether coming or going. In his view, it is a sign that sanctifies the most ordinary of activities: putting on shoes, taking a bath, sharing meals, and even lighting a candle. Applied to our own day, there is nothing wrong with making this sign in our cars at the beginning or ending of a trip, in an airplane at takeoff or landing, or else getting on or off any form of public transportation. It is pious practice to make the sign to thank God for good news or to ask for help when we find ourselves in the face of danger. Whether we are on the way home or headed out for the day, relaxing in our chairs or going to work, getting up in the morning or going to bed; no matter what, he says, "we make the Sign of the Cross."[38]

The visible gesture signifies an invisible reality, the spiritual relationship between the Christian and the Risen Lord (see CCC 1235). In the West, this is done by extending the fingers of one's open right hand to touch first the forehead, then just below the chest, then from the left shoulder to the right before folding one's hands in prayer. This action is accompanied by an invocation of the Trinity with the words, "In the Name of the Father, and of the Son, and of the Holy Spirit. Amen."

---

[38] My own paraphrased translation of De Corona Militis 3: "Ad omnem progressum atque promotum, ad omnem ditum et exitum, ad uestitum, ad calciatum, ad lauacra, ad mensas, ad lumina, ad cubilia, ad sedilia, qua cumque nos conversatio exercet, frontem signaculo terimus."

The sign is meant to solicit faith even in the face of difficult doubts. What is visible and physical is established in relation to what is invisible and spiritual. Tracing one's fingers from head to gut could be understood to indicate how our salvation extends from the highest to the most humble of human activities, from the most spiritual powers of the soul to the very core of our bodily existence.[39] As we touch from one shoulder and cross over to the other, it is as if we are declaring that the power of our faith extends out to everything that is within the horizon of humanity to master, command, possess, influence, protect, and love.

The Seal of Our Heart

The Fathers of the Church called the Sign of the Cross a *seal*, and we could add that it is like a "seal of the heart" (Song of Songs 8:6). In fact, the action forms a cross over our whole body, in the center of which is our heart. The heart is not only a physiological center of life for our body, but it speaks to a spiritual center of our very being. The deepest center of our personal existence, the place where we should be most at rest with ourselves, is the place where the Lord speaks to us.

For those who seek to live with themselves, the Sign of the Cross indicates the very threshold to our innermost sanctuary.

---

[39] Olivier Clement describes three spiritual centers in the human person discussed by the Eastern Church Fathers: the *nous* or the mind, the seat of the intellect at the forehead; the *epithumus* or gut instincts, centered in the belly; and the *thumus* or the heart, the seat of tender affectivity where God speaks. See *The Roots of Christian Mysticism: Texts from the Patristic Era with Commentary*, trans. Theodore Berkeley and Hummerstone (New York: New City Press, 2002), 134.

Under this sign, an overflowing fountain of mercy springs up within us, bathing our wounds of sin and making us whole. In the depths of a heart sealed by the Cross, God is waiting to reveal His love.

The ancient monks understood the importance of *habitare secum*. This means learning to live with ourselves, and it includes deliberation from the depth of our being about who we are and what we really want. Those who want to pray must go there: every good, true, and noble love is conceived there before it is given birth in words and actions.

All manner of wickedness is also conceived there and constantly threatens to overthrow the greatness of human dignity —and our prayer must also learn to submit this darkness to the Lord as well. The Cross of Christ in this case points to and safeguards what is most tender and good about our humanity. This is true even in the face of our interior poverty and weakness so that what the delicate work God has begun in us might reach completion.

Is this corporal movement really so important for our life of prayer? The profound and mysterious relationships between body and soul, physical gesture and spiritual contemplation, the exterior day-to-day affairs of human life and the internal spiritual truths that sustain it come together in the Sign of the Cross.

Saint Athanasius describes this sign as an action of faith that opens up a true contemplation of the world. He explains that through this action the eye of faith raises its vision, from this visible world below to the heavens above. In so doing, this sacred gesture renews our awareness of the victory of the Risen Lord over the powers of sin and death.[40]

---

[40] See Saint Athanasius, *On the Incarnation* 31, 32.

This gesture of devotion disposes our hearts to live by spiritual faith. Under the Cross, every worldly power and selfish ambition is seen for what it is. This sign submits what is below to what is above, the earthly reality of our lives to the heavenly reality of God's life.

In the face of the evils afflicting this life, it takes faith to believe that God is almighty and concerned about our plight. In this life, faith alone sees the definitive triumph of good over evil. Yet even when life's ambiguities seem impossible, this sign points us in the right direction and reminds us of those truths from above that we see only obscurely as in a mirror in this life. Under this blessing, fire can flash down from heaven, mountains can be moved, and the hearts of men, otherwise closed, can be laid bare.

Not only does the Cross lead us within ourselves but we also call it to mind because it defines our relationships with one another, revealing who we are before God and the world. When we make the Sign of the Cross we affirm our ecclesial identity as members of the Body of Christ, part of a people who find themselves at a crossroads, who have the opportunity to turn back to God. Making this sign is also a constant reminder that we are in the world, but not of it: the mystery of the Cross invoked by this simple gesture binds Christians, rejected, misunderstood, and persecuted, to love even their enemies with gentle kindness and never to be impatient in working for the salvation of all.

The Sacred Bond between God and the Christian

The Sign of the Cross is a blessing, a sacramental (see CCC 1078, 1671). This mean it signifies a renewal of that sacred bond between the believer and God established by Christ crucified, and also to each another in the secret of our faith. As a sacramental, this sign binds us to liturgy, our holy service before the Lord.

The term *sacramental*, like the word *sacrament*, derives from the Latin *sacramentum*—originally a sacred oath by which the ancient Romans bound themselves to friends and countrymen in service to one another. Such agreements were based on a common understanding of piety and loyalty not shared by their enemies. The Church took over this term to interpret the biblical Greek *mysterion*. The biblical idea of mystery refers to invisible, spiritual power. Such a mystery is defined by a hidden wisdom and secret identity that the Lord entrusts to those whom He has especially bound to Himself. To live out this *sacramentum*, this *mysterion*, means to have the courage and humility to trust the Lord, to rely on Him for what is truly essential.

This kind of intimacy with the Lord is possible only by grace, which binds us to Him. Grace is the gift of participating in the life of Christ. We are bound to Christ by His life in us. The grace of Christ comes objectively, or *ex opera operato*, through the seven sacraments. This means that baptism, confirmation, Eucharist, confession, anointing of the sick, holy orders, and marriage are actions of Christ that bind us to Him, whatever our dispositions.

So objectively present is the grace of Christ in the sacraments that if we attempt to receive one of these sacraments unworthily, we bring on our own condemnation by our abuse of His love. On the other hand, if we are obedient to Christ and humbly confident in His love, Christ's action in the sacraments takes up our devotion and incorporates us deeper and deeper into His Mystery. This is true above all in the Eucharist.

Grace is also given in other sacred actions and holy things established by the Church that are called *sacramentals*. These actions and things subjectively avail our hearts to the grace of Christ's action rather than objectively cause its effects. This means sacramentals, including the Sign of the Cross, dispose us to a deeper relationship with Christ when we perform them with true devotion.

Although they are distinct, it would be a serious mistake to fail to see the relationship between sacraments and sacramentals. In the life of Christian prayer, this is a necessary relationship. The seven sacraments as well as all sacramentals are ordered to Christ by the power of the Holy Spirit for the increase of grace. Prompted and produced by the Holy Spirit, these channels of grace do not stand separate and isolated from one another, but permeate prayer like living realities.

Sacramentals, including sacred images, blessed elements such as holy water, and many other venerable things and blessings find their source and summit in the Eucharist. Through these, Christ's gift of Himself at Mass is called to mind in all circumstances and situations, even those in which the Lord seems mysteriously absent. In other words, something about sacramentals in general and the Sign of the Cross in particular, can reawaken the same devotion for Christ in our hearts. We ought to have this devotion when we receive Holy Communion. This spiritual movement of love renews and in a sense extends that sacred moment here and now in this particular situation.

At the same time, the liturgies in which sacraments are conferred include many different sacramentals through which the whole assembly together participates in manifold ways according to their liturgical functions. Among the sacramentals that makes such participation conscious, the Sign of the Cross (which we have already seen is a contemplative gesture) is arguably the most prominent.

The point is that when a baptized person performs an act of worship such as the Sign of the Cross, the whole liturgical dimension of his existence manifests itself. Making the Sign of the Cross before and after meals or when we begin to travel deepens one's participation in the sacraments of the Church. This simple gesture of piety permeates one's day-to-day life with the presence of the Lord.

The Holy Spirit works in incalculable ways to bind us to Christ more deeply at any given moment so that no matter what we are doing or where we are, we always have time and space for God. Sacraments and sacramentals, both actions of faith and devotion, are ordered to one another as complementary manifestations of God's love, each flowing from and leading to the other. It is as impossible to have one without the other as it is to have faith without devotion, or love for God without love of neighbor.

6

THE SIGN OF THE CROSS
AND OUR BAPTISM

The Sign of the Cross has a special connection to baptism. It is traced by the Church on the forehead of the catechumen before baptism. It is a sign that this life has been brought under the shadow of Christ's work of redemption. It marks the soul as the Lord's special possession and erases all absolute claims any principality or power attempt to make over it.

Whenever we make this sign, we renew our baptismal promises. These promises include the rejection of Satan, his work, and his empty promises. Without Christ, we are under our adversary's rule, implicated in his work, and deceived to act against our own integrity.

By blessing ourselves, we renew our declaration of freedom and defiance in the face of evil. It is our visible profession that we have died to ourselves in the waters of baptism and that we have been raised up with new life not subject to the devil's dominion. We choose instead to live by faith in Christ Jesus and declare that the fruit of His obedience has triumphed over the power of sin in us.

Extending the Cross from our head to our gut, from shoulder to shoulder is a disavowal of every project and design that would tear down, confuse, deceive, and foment hostility to human dignity and life. This sacred gesture declares that we will not implicate ourselves or our resources to anything that will diminish the dignity of our neighbor or ourselves. We signify our resolve that evil work will have no place in our lives, even if this means having to suffer great evil and humiliation for the sake of Christ.

The gesture of the Cross and the invocation of the Trinity repudiate Satan's every suggestion that we can achieve something good by doing something evil. By this sign we rise up and stake our lives of the promises of the living God. This sign renews our pledge to take our stand on what is good, beautiful, and true.

The promises that we renew by this sign of blessing also include the decision to stand up for and live by the Holy Trinity. This sign affirms that we believe that the God who reveals Himself as Father, Son, and Holy Spirit has revealed not an appearance, but the fullness of the divine mystery itself. It is not an appearance that rectifies our being, but our dignity finds its footing the mystery of God Himself.

When we bless ourselves, we affirm that above the heavens and below the earth, the Uncreated Love of the Trinity circumscribes and holds together everything visible and invisible. Our blessing renews our commitment to live by love and die by love. We signify with this sign that we have pledged our lives, our honor, and everything we hold dear to affirm this truth about God to our last breath.

To renew our pledge to the Trinity through this sign does not mean we simply believe the Trinity exists or what the Trinity has revealed; we also believe for the sake of God, because we love Him. If we love Him, we love all those He has created in His wondrous love. The Sign of the Cross renews this solemn devotion. Ending with "Amen," a declaration of truth before God (see CCC 1061–1065), we renew our irrevocable pledge of devotion to Him, and acknowledge that He is ever devoted to us.

A Sign of Protection

The saints use the Sign of the Cross as a shield, a protection against all evil, all diabolical irrationality. As she grew into spiritual maturity through prayer, Saint Teresa of Ávila came to understand the importance of this sign. In fact, the first part of her *Interior Castle* suggests that if we do not enter more deeply into our hearts by disciplined prayer, we are unnecessarily vulnerable to antihuman spiritual forces.

She describes such forces as poisonous snakes, toads, and lizards that are always trying to frighten us away from a true encounter with the Lord. They are constantly trying to undermine our faith. She advocates making the Sign of the Cross as a sure way to stand firm against their attacks on our trust in God. She simply assumes that this physical action has spiritual power to deepen our confidence in such times of trial.

Going back even further, Saint Anthony of the Desert, a third-century Egyptian hermit, also encouraged the Sign of the Cross. He used it to combat all kinds of confusion, terror, deception, depression, frustration, nostalgia, discouragement, and contention and a long list of other vexations that often haunt those who take up the battle to pray.[41] Dehumanizing irrationality is rendered powerless when exposed to the divine rationality of God's love revealed in the Cross.

---

[41] See Saint Athanasius, *Life of Anthony and the Letter to Marcellinus,* trans. Robert C. Gregg, Classics of Western Spirituality (Mahwah, NJ: Paulist Press, 1980), 41, 48.

Saint Athanasius explains in his *Life of Antony* that the ancient forces that oppose what is genuinely human are in fact irrational and are powerless in the face of the truth. That is why they always work on the level of deception—misrepresenting the facts to confuse, seduce, and discourage. When we do nothing to defend ourselves against their efforts to pull us into their dark swamps of demented reasoning, we soon find ourselves engaged in self-destructive activities.

The Sign in Spiritual Combat

Forsaking the physical and bodily dimension of our prayer can have perilous consequences. If we do not use our bodies as instruments of grace and sanctify them by holy gestures and words, we are more inclined to allow ourselves to be duped into self-destructive practices. When we do not realize that our faith is not simply a nice idea or religious fantasy to think about during the holidays, then, in the difficult grind of day-to-day existence, our tormented spirits will come to see the body as a burden and its destruction as a means of escape.

The demonic is very real. We should not be overly curious about it, but we should not be indifferent either. I asked one young person why she was cutting herself. She explained to me that it was the only relief that she could find from the pain that burdened her heart. The idea to do this was not something that she thought of on her own. It was suggested to her in her own mind while she was by herself. She could not recognize the demonic deception, and the physical self-abuse seemed to work—for a while. Yet this only led to a greater sense of alienation and inclination to self-destruction. By herself, she was unable learn how to combat this kind of thinking. She needed the help of others, in whom she could confide and who would help her discern.

This kind of spiritual attack involves not only an increasingly common psychological pathology, but also illustrates that our minds and bodies are connected. If we do not respect this connection, we are open to all kinds of dangers—psychological, physiological, and spiritual. As happened to this young lady, evil spirits want to rob humanity of its trust in God and in others; for without trust in God's love, even the youngest and brightest among us are subject to every irrational impulse. In addition to getting young people to trained counselors to help them deal with the events that dispose them to this behavior and having the courage to enter into their hearts, it is also helpful to give them spiritual signs that they can offer with their bodies.

In the face of this, the Sign of the Cross is a physical reminder of God's love for humanity and the greatness of human dignity that flows from this love. It connects our bodily life here below with the heavenly life from above. When the Christian mindfully blesses himself with faith, the reason to trust God is signified with the body. A soul grounded in such trust and rooted deeply in the truth can be tried by all kinds of malicious falsehood, but as long as it remains under the Sign of the Cross, it can never be overcome.

In the age of chivalry, Saint Dominic would also arm himself with the Sign of the Cross. Before any prayerful study of the Bible or the Fathers of the Church, he would bless himself. As he marched miles and miles to preach the gospel, he would sign himself so frequently that he looked as if he were swatting flies.[42]

---

[42] See *Early Dominicans: Selected Writings*, ed. Fr. Simon Tugwell, O.P., Classics of Western Spirituality: A Library of Great Spiritual Masters (Mahwah, NJ: Paulist Press, 1982), 101–102.

To study the Word of God prayerfully and to preach it to others requires that we enter into a vulnerable place where thoughts opposed to God can sometimes assail us. These come from dehumanizing forces both within and beyond our own psychology. Whatever their source, they want to oppose us and discourage our efforts.

Making the Sign of the Cross deliberately and with faith protects us from any suggestion that prayer is a waste of time, or something to put off until later, or else something to become proud over. These kinds of thoughts are, after all, demonic ideas, ideas in direct opposition to the reality of prayer. When we bless ourselves with this sign, these falsehoods are revealed against the prayer offered for us by the One who was crucified by love.

The Sign of Courage

For most Christians, especially the persecuted and those who are facing death, this sign is an occasion of hope and a source of strength. We make this sign as an expression of solidarity with all those who have gone before us marked by the sign of faith. It is the sign of our common forefathers in the faith — of countless men and women who courageously accepted every trial, persecution, rejection, imprisonment, torture, and even death. Their complete trust in the Holy Trinity, all the way to the end, helps us to see the truth of God's love. Thus, when we make the sign of blessing that they made before us, we too find the courage to accept this blessing and to stand firm in our faith.

Making the Sign of the Cross involves the decision to choose the Cross as one's standard in life. The sign is a reminder that every decision and action ought to be a response to the love the Lord revealed on the Cross. This love is a true sacrificial love, and to respond, one must be ready to make real sacrifices of love in the circumstances of one's life. In the face of this reality, all one's actions are endowed with a spiritual meaning.

That which one does in his body, through his actions and the movements of his heart, and also what he fails to do, is either an acceptance or rejection of the love expressed in the Sign of the Cross. Thus, when we make this sign, not only with our hand but also with the intention of our heart and the attention of our mind, we begin to pray, not only with our bodies but also our spirits. In this way, Christian prayer is meant to be profoundly whole — body and soul, affection and thought, heart and understanding. Such prayer leads to courage, the movement toward reconciliation with God, the beginning of a pilgrimage to our Father's house.

7

THE PRIMACY OF GRACE

Prayer is a sacred conversation with God.[43] In this conversation, God truly listens to us, and we must learn to listen to Him. By faith, we can hear the Word of the Father speaking into the silence of our existence. Moreover, He in whom the Father abides is eagerly waiting for us to respond in the image and likeness of His perfect fullness. He has given us the Holy Spirit so that we might call out with Him what He commanded us to pray, "Abba, Father!"

The Word who is God reveals everything that the Father has to say to us. What more can we desire? No matter how much we take in, there is always more to learn. No matter how much we understand, we become aware of an even greater love and tenderness that we do not understand. No matter how much we respond, there is always more than our words can say. When His Word is welcomed into our silenced poverty, our poor silence is filled with His every blessing.

This kind of prayer, however, requires us to seek help from above. Although we have natural capacities for prayer and we are essentially religious beings, our natural inclinations toward God are never enough for the conversation that He longs to

[43] See Origen, *De Oratione* 3.

share with us. Without help from above, our effort to connect with the One who is above us always falls short.

To say that we are essentially religious beings means that we cannot be happy if we do not seek the One who is above this world and learn to praise Him. Nothing in this world below is sufficient to enable us to answer the high calling that we have received. Nothing subject to visible, material, and physical reality is commensurate with the desire of our hearts. How can we desire what is eternal if we are creatures simply subject to change in matter and the law of entropy? To realize what we are created to be requires assistance above and beyond the limits of physical and visible reality.

Endowed with a dignity too great for this world to hold, we are in the world but not of it. The material world, wonderful and necessary as it is for this life, is too small for the great things that live in our hearts. By our own waning powers, we can grasp those good things that we see in the here and now for but a short time. Whatever we achieve for ourselves by our own industry eventually perishes and fades away. Yet, deep in our hearts, we burn for something that cannot fade.

Because we are embodied spiritual creatures by divine design, our lives remain only half-lived until we encounter the One in whose image and likeness we are fashioned. When our hearts are raised above their natural capacities, prayer orders all that is physical and visible in this world below to what is invisible and spiritual in the world above.

Calling to us, each by name, He awaits us with love and mercy. We hide in the shadows of our lives as prodigals, dishonest servants, disgruntled laborers, Pharisees, demoniacs, adulterers, prostitutes, murderers, and thieves. Born blind to glory, deaf to wisdom, mute to the truth, we are imprisoned crippled beggars whose eyes, ears, and mouths can be opened by the Liberator who comes for us.

Filling this very moment with a fullness of life, the divine Neighbor is passing by disguised in unfamiliar comeliness. Although we have been too indifferent to the plight of our neighbors, His heart is pierced when He finds us left for dead on the road of life. When will we come to our senses, reach out to Him, and cry for mercy?

Our natural religiosity is limited. There are truths that we need to live life to the full, but without divine assistance, we can at best come to know them only partially and after a lifetime of effort. This is why the Father spoke His Word into our flesh — so that we might know the truth and live life to the full.

Until we learn to trust everything the Lord has revealed about Himself, we are vulnerable to all kinds of hubris and self-deception, or else disappointment and despair. After all, left to my own devices, how do I know whether my conversation with God ever goes beyond any more than a monologue with myself? Many have made a shipwreck of their faith because they are blown off course by the winds of false myths and erroneous teaching.

The Church and Divine Authority

When it comes to the truth about prayer, the Church hands on what Christ handed on to her when He gave Himself up for her to make her holy and immaculate in His presence (see Eph. 5:25–27). Christian tradition proposes with divine authority that God desires to give us the grace to pray in ways that truly connect us to Him when we ask with faith and perseverance. The Church boldly proclaims that Christ the Lord gives a real access to that which is above.

Her sacred doctrine affirms that He is the great High Priest whose entry into the heavenly sanctuary renders our prayers acceptable to God. She sees Him as the Lamb of God, slain but risen from the dead, reigning on the throne of grace over all things. She invites us to pray the way He commands, and through her ministry, we are given the grace we need to obey Him.

A Supernatural Gift

With the Gift of the Holy Spirit, the gift of supernatural grace makes one's whole existence holy. This doctrine of *deification*, or *divinization*, involves a true sharing in God's life that does not diminish our created dignity but raises our freedom above its natural capacities. To be assimilated into the life of God in a way that perfects our humanity, the human person, as a creature, needs a gift that elevates, transforms, and unites it to the Holy Trinity. Sanctifying grace given through a new presence of the Holy Spirit in the soul is a participation in the life of God in the sense that it implicates and lifts up the very substance and nature of what it means to be a human being in the very life of God.

The theological tradition says that this sharing in divine life has a *physical*, *formal*, *analogous*, and *accidental* character.[44] This seems odd to affirm and can easily be misunderstood. A proper understanding of these terms, however, opens up the mystery of sanctifying grace and protects it from dangerous and reductionistic lines of reasoning.

We say that grace is an *accidental* participation in the life of God because even those who do not know God and who have rejected grace still have a soul and remain in the Divine Image.

---

[44] See Jordan Aumann, *Spiritual Theology* (London: Continuum, 1980, 2006), 69.

Whether or not someone has the gift of grace, his life is sacred and his dignity calls for respect. Furthermore, sanctifying grace does not physically change a human being into a wholly different creature. Human nature receives the life of God as a secondary reality, a second nature. This means that grace builds up and perfects humanity but does not replace it. This also means that as we accept the gift of grace, our frailty and inadequacy do not magically disappear. Instead, through grace we discover in our weaknesses that the power of God is brought to perfection (see 2 Cor. 12:9).

Why do we affirm that grace is an *analogous* participation in divine life? *Analogous* refers to the true relation, the harmony, the due proportion that grace establishes between creatures and God. Grace does not make us God by nature. If it did, we would cease to be human; we would cease to be at all. There would be no question of harmony or relation between humanity and divinity, between creation and creator.

To be *analogous*, to be in harmony, to be in due proportion requires that the soul who freely accepts sanctifying grace perfects its unique individuality before God. Affirming that grace is an analogous participation in the life of God is therefore essential for understanding justification. Grace, because it is analogous, gives real standing before God, because without standing there is no real relation. The gift of God is an analogous participation in the life of God insofar as it brings new and deeper meaning to the personal existence of the believer, establishing a real relation, while animating, healing, and perfecting the uniqueness of the individual before the Lord.

The more infused our humanity is with divine life, the greater our union with God and at the same time, the more fully human we become. Grace makes us *like* God to unite us to Him.

This increased likeness does not diminish our humanity, and our union with God does not deprive us of our freedom. Instead the closer we draw to God, the greater freedom we enjoy, and the more we are like Him, the more the uniqueness of who we are delights His heart.

An analogous participation in God's life opens up an understanding of relational mysticism that stands over and against various mysticisms of identity. Many systems propose an absolute being or absolute emptiness that either absorbs or annihilates the individual soul. In pantheistic systems, like that proposed by Hegel, the value of the individual is only its part in an overall process. Here, a measurable outcome yet to be realized surmounts the uniqueness of the individual: no soul is to be saved, but instead individual freedom must be overcome, made to conform. Our participation in God's life, on the contrary, is not about mere compliance, but about a tender friendship with God, a sacred solidarity with the whole reality of heaven.

What do theologians mean by the term *physical?* In this context, *physical* does not mean simply something visible or bodily or material but instead refers to something invisible and spiritual. Grace works not extrinsic to the soul's natural powers, but intrinsically through them, renewing the soul's very substance. God's nature does not impose itself from without but lifts up and expands the soul's interiority so that the Divine Persons might dwell in it.

To participate *physically* in the life of God implies that the soul can be animated by a life infinitely deeper and fuller than the one that is its own by nature. It can have a second nature, a new nature within its nature, a life that is "not my own" (cf. Gal. 2:20). In the life of grace, frail human nature is physically caught up in and transformed by the immensity of divine life.

How is grace a *formal* participation in divine life? The form of grace is divine — it comes from God and is in God, not man. To say participation in divine life is formal affirms that the grace that makes us holy is a higher reality, above our human nature, capable of lifting our created nature into the very life of God. Divine life is a gift that is over the soul, above human existence, and its divine form lifts the soul above the limits of human nature without harming the integrity of our humanity. To say that grace is a physical and formal participation in the life of God is to say that all that is most noble, good, and true about being human is under the influence of this higher power.

This kind of participation in divine life subordinates everything that can be felt and touched, understood and imagined in human existence so that nothing can separate us from the love of God. New powers of faith, hope, and love, infused virtues, and an array of spiritual gifts lift merely human works above themselves. The grace that makes us holy elevates, transforms, and unites to God that part of us that is deeper than our bodily existence and even our psychological powers, so that through cooperation with the Holy Spirit, we can actually give praise to God. Thus, grace as a *physical* and *formal* sharing in God's life refers to those depths and horizons of human existence and being that no science can adequately measure or examine.

Sanctifying grace involves the deepest center of the soul, reaching deeper into our human substance than any feeling, any enlightened state of consciousness, or any attitude, although it can influence all of this in the powers of the soul. This gift of holiness is an intrinsic principle at work within our nature: not an external force, not an extrinsic influence, not a power imposed over and against the natural greatness of humanity. In the very center of our being is where God physically implicates our frail human "I" with His omnipotent divine "Thou," tenderly setting apart the very substance of who we are, subtly consecrating our very life-principle itself so that we can offer our bodies as a living sacrifice of praise.

In the form of heavenly things, the grace that makes us holy involves a sacrificial self-emptying of our humanity and a divinely humble lifting up of our frailties. Not limiting itself to the greatest and most powerful, the perfection of this eternal life is revealed in our weakness and failures. It is not the product of human effort or industry, but of trust and complete surrender. Only Uncreated Love can create this new life in the soul, but to do so, the soul must die to itself out of devotion to its crucified Master.

Through this blessing from above, God reveals His glory while protecting the integrity of human nature. Sanctifying grace raises the wonder of human dignity, helping man and woman see the greatness of each one's created purpose. This gift from above commits the saint more deeply to promoting what is good and noble in the created order even as he is drawn closer to the Lord's uncreated mystery.

A New Start for Humanity

Grace does not destroy or diminish, but instead heals and perfects all that is good, holy, and true about our humanity. This gift establishes a new relation of love and life between Creator and creature. From the furthest periphery of our flesh-imbued soul unto the deepest substance of our embodied spirit, this share in the life of God is at work animating all that is genuine and true in each believer's humanity with the warmth of Divine Love and glows in the light of eternal truth.

In this new life from above, my prayer discovers the space I need to let go of my own projects and plans so that I can embrace

God's plan with my own freedom—which He cherishes and awaits, but never forces. The greater this union, the more completely His work of creation is perfected in me, the more fully I discover the greatness of who I really am. Sanctifying grace raises my uniqueness into harmony and right relation with the mystery of God.

Those who believe in Christ Jesus and the salvation He won for them are established in this inexhaustible treasury of love won for them on the Cross. He has already paid the price to give them this freedom. By his grace, whatever they have done and whatever the circumstances they face, they can raise their prayer, and the countless unspoken prayers of this whole broken world, above the limits of our frail humanity and up into the heart of God.

Grace is our participation in the life of God. This participation in the wisdom and love exchanged by the Divine Persons in the unity of the Trinity characterizes Christian prayer. It is the eternal Son who prays to the Father in the Holy Spirit when a Christian lifts up his heart to give thanks in the mystery of our faith.

Christ's prayer in history continues now in mystery. By supernatural grace, the desires of the Lord unleashed in his earthly prayer are not a historically distant reality to which we merely provide our intellectual assent. His living desires are the source of all Christian desire in prayer. What burns so worthily in His Heart burns away all that is unworthy in ours. What moves Him to cry out from His Heart to the Father also raises up everything that is good, holy, and true in us. Doing everything in our power to make ourselves vulnerable to feel what the Lord feels and think what the Lord thinks allows us to make His desire in prayer our own and our desires His.

FIRE FROM ABOVE

The Primacy of Grace in Prayer

Arguing for the primacy of grace in prayer today is important because we live in a time of "self-help" books. Such works often offer little more than fantastic hubris when it comes to the spiritual life. No human wisdom can replace what only a living relationship with the Risen Lord provides.

Christ renews our minds and changes our thinking by sanctifying grace—a gift by which we participate in the very life of God. Grace causes a living encounter with the Lord. It is a pure and undeserved gift that flows from the heart of Him who was pierced for our offenses and is risen from the dead. Divinely endowed, this new life permeates and raises the very substance of our soul, making the inner essence of our humanity holy in the sight of God.

Even when the spiritual life involves difficult renunciation or persevering through an impossible trial, the reason such heroism is possible is because of the grace of Christ. Every Christian knows that when he is really tested, it is only God's grace that sees him through. His power is made perfect in our weakness, and in the end all glory and honor belong to Him alone.

Consider the father who went to Jesus for his son's sake in the Gospel of Mark. His son was afflicted with a deadly spirit that caused irrational and dangerous behavior. He wanted Jesus' help, but because his son's misery seemed insurmountable, he was not unconditionally confident in his petition. What parent can fail to identify with this paternal anxiety?

Jesus was able to answer this anxiety because He fully understands every heart that comes to him. He hears our most secret sorrows and feels our emptiness because He has entered into the same mud from which we are made. In the face of the father's plight, He did the most loving thing he could do. Jesus discreetly admonished the distressed father for his disbelief. The doubt that up to that moment had plagued the father's heart was laid bare.

Until his doubt was recognized, the man was not free to have faith, the kind of faith he needed for his son's sake. His own dignity as the father of his son was impaired by his self-ignorance. Jesus' word, however, helped the man see the truth. We are ever vulnerable to all kinds of irrational spirits because of our lack of trust in God.

This gentle rebuke stirred the man to the kind of faith he needed. The word of Christ helped him humbly recognize the dehumanizing lack of faith from which he suffered and, with this recognition, to find the courage to submit his doubt to the Lord. A confident and truthful prayer emerged from the depths of his heart, "I believe; help my unbelief!" (Mark 9:24).

Conversatio Morum

To welcome the Eternal Word like this means a commitment to Saint Benedict's ancient *conversatio morum*—this ongoing dialogue with God that takes up our whole existence, our whole manner of life, all our judgments, all our dreams, all our desires. It renders all of this vulnerable to the secret things of God, His divine being, His life, His inscrutable judgments, His divine dream and eternal plan. Prayer brings together things so unfamiliar in themselves: human limitedness with divine limitlessness, our frailty with His omnipotence, our misery with His mercy.

To have faith in our crucified God means to let Him question us about the restlessness of our hearts, about the burden of guilt we carry, and about the mystery of death with which we wrestle. Our hope in Him helps us rediscover ourselves through the loving eyes of the One who has conquered sin and death. Truly to encounter the Word of God is to allow Him to reveal the boundless love of the Father, to allow ourselves to be loved immeasurably in the light of this self-disclosure, and to be open to the desire to repay this excessive love with our own frail love —no matter how inadequate our effort.

This conversation with God involves a supernatural receptivity and attentiveness to the Lord. This means we cannot really listen to God without help from above. In prayer, the sacred doctrine of the Church opens up the mystery of God's revelation to establish and protect our personal integrity and dignity. In prayer, the heart-piercing ways Christ has loved us can renew the hope we have inside. In prayer, the challenge of being obedient to the Word of God can make us fecund with the love that created the world.

The next three chapters explore the work of grace in our intellect, in our affections and memory, and in our will. Our powers to think and understand become holy through the gift of supernatural faith. God sets apart our emotional powers and self-awareness through supernatural hope. Our wills desire what God wills through the love that comes from Him. Through these theological virtues our psychological powers are set ablaze by His fire in us. They purify and enlarge a kind of sacred space in the depths of our being. Divesting us of everything that prevents us from hearing His voice, these gifts allow our hearts to burn inside as He journeys with us on the way.

8

FAITH AND TRUST

To begin, we will argue that in order to have a conversation with the Lord, we need to trust what the Church proposes to us in Scripture and Tradition. This sacred doctrine protects us from the extreme individualism and hostility toward God that marks our times. Conversation with God does not violate the integrity of our faith but brings to bear what the Church teaches into our effort to attend to His voice and respond to His Word.

Faith is much more than an intellectual assent to a body of propositions but instead provides the very substance of our hope. After arguing for the importance of trusting the teaching of the Church, we will argue that sacred doctrine opens us up to a heart-piercing encounter with Christ. The Bible and Tradition do not merely propose ideas about God, but God meets us in them. The normal response to this personal encounter in prayer is compunction, the gift of tears. The more we look to God as our hope, the deeper our conversation with Him goes.

The Wisdom of the Spanish Doctors of the Church

At the threshold of the sixteenth century, there was a mystical explosion. Not unlike the explosion of prayer unfolding in our time, a number of men and women were moved to engage the Lord in a deep exchange of hearts. This eruption of holiness coincided with the discovery of America, the reconquest of Spain, and the rebirth of Spanish higher education in the arts and humanities. As wonderful as these accomplishments and discoveries have been for Western Civilization, the faith, hope, and love discovered through the conversation with God has imparted an even greater and more lasting spiritual patrimony to humanity.

Three Doctors of the Church are especially noted for their teaching on prayer who helped shape this spiritual renewal in Spain. What each of them has in common is the conviction that conversation with God involves a personal encounter with the Lord that can be properly understood only through the teaching of the Church. Their writings on prayer are all informed by sound doctrine and are rich with scriptural images.

The great teacher, Saint John of Ávila, is called the Apostle of Andalusia. His preaching converted many of Spain's greatest saints. When his health was failing, Saint Ignatius of Loyola commanded his brethren in Spain to take care of him, commenting that his command of Sacred Scripture was so great that his death would be a great loss for the Church. Saint John identifies the teaching of the Church and the Holy Bible, and he is convinced that God speaks through this sacred doctrine. His great spiritual classic *Audi Filia* presents Psalm 45:11–12 as God's teaching the Church how to attract Christ to herself: "Listen, O Daughter, and See."

This vital connection between doctrine and prayer was an important part of the Carmelite Reform. In a later chapter we will provide a more thorough exploration of some of the teachings of Saint John of the Cross. For purposes of this discussion it is enough simply to observe his tremendous command of Sacred Scripture. Saint John of the Cross argues how a soul ought to conduct itself as it enters into communion with God based on what the Church proposes in the Bible.

His most important poems are filled with subtle scriptural allusions unpacked and further developed in his commentary. Doctrine is not an obstacle to the deep mystery of Christian prayer, but Church teaching provided a basis for him to discuss the unfathomable splendors that bathe a soul in this conversation with God. In all of this, however, he is merely following in the footsteps of the first pioneer of the Carmelite Reform—at once his spiritual mother and daughter, Saint Teresa of Ávila.

Teresa of Ávila was not merely born into Spanish culture— Spanish culture, its deepest and most vital center, was in many ways given birth by her. Among his most important works, Saint John of Ávila affirmed Saint Teresa when she wrote him seeking confirmation for her own approach to prayer. Like him, she understood that sacred doctrine and prayer needed to be integrated. Through the integration that she realized, the fire of mental prayer infused and marked the Spanish soul. Spanish culture even today is impenetrable if her spiritual contributions are overlooked.

Hidden from view, transformative, astonishing, both conquistadors and bishops found themselves immersed in hushed adoration because of her witness, her writings, and her friends. This fire of love unvanquished drove her far beyond the limits of frail health. She wanted people to pray completely open to mystical wisdom, an understanding flowing from the heart of the Church, a living knowledge that the Bride guards for her Bridegroom.

Her own spiritual writings are vital because she immersed herself in the writings of other mystics on fire with the love of God. She soon discovered, however, the need for discernment.

She herself was hindered in her own spiritual growth by bad teaching.

The practice of mental prayer without conscious adherence to the teaching of the Church left many very vulnerable to serious errors. Some spiritual people asserted their personal authority and experience above the Scriptures and Tradition of the Church. These errors sometimes caused people to act against the unity of the Church and their own personal integrity.

The reaction of many was to regard mental prayer or conversation with God as something dangerous. Some theologians argued that only the most disciplined contemplatives should dare risk this effort. For the rest of the faithful, liturgical and vocal forms of devotions would suffice as long as they lived good moral lives.

Against this, Saint Teresa of Ávila proposed that mental prayer was a conversation with God that should be carried out by everyone in the Church who wants to please God. She was familiar with the new spiritual exercises and understanding of mental prayer among her contemporaries. Looking to Saint John of Ávila and other saints of the time as a reference, she understood that these new approaches to prayer needed to be rooted in the teaching of the Church.

Her greater spiritual masterpiece is *Interior Castle*. She describes the soul as a kind of crystal globe that glows with a beautiful light shining from its very center. The light is the Holy Trinity, Who dwells in this crystal sphere as if in the center of a castle. The soul magnifies this light, shining in the darkness of the world.

The soul itself is beautifully arranged with various levels of dwelling places — some more interior and some more exterior. The more interior chambers are the more beautiful until, in the very center, one beholds the beauty of God's presence itself radiating through it all. Without this radiating presence, the soul becomes nothing more than a dark shell and crumbles into nothing.

Although she has many descriptions about experiences that she has had in prayer, it would be a reductionistic reading to conclude that she is chiefly concerned with providing descriptions of spiritual or psychological experiences. Her whole work is constructed around the objective presence of God by grace.

The doctrine of the Church concerning God's presence in the soul is the vital foundation for Saint Teresa's observations on prayer. Her writings presume belief in the God of the Bible, who knows, creates, and sustains the soul's existence. She argues from the Church's teaching that through Christ's work of redemption, faith in Him opens up the possibility of a new kind of divine presence in the soul by grace. It is faith in the Word made flesh that allows the Trinity to shine in the soul in a saving and sanctifying way so that we might personally love and know Him.

In Saint Teresa's spiritual doctrine, we are not saved or sanctified by spiritual experiences, but God's transforming presence makes itself known and felt through experiences. Prayer is about a real personal and mutual connection with God. For Saint Teresa, our connection with God, who dwells within, is not realized through psychological experiences but by His presence as it is proposed by our faith. It is through what we believe, rather than the experiences we have, that we are more deeply connected to Him.

Mental prayer is made possible and begins when we believe that God is personally present to us in a way that the Church proposes in her teaching. He is the light that shines in the darkness of our lives, the warmth that prevents us from being overcome by the coldness of this world. To believe what the Church proposes about the Trinity in the soul through faith in Christ is the only way for us to render the personal response this divine presence evokes, the only way for us to have a true conversation with God.

If we confuse conversation with God with the pursuit of spiritual experiences, we are on a path away from a conversatio morum. No matter how deep one adheres to the Lord by faith, he is never in this life in a place where he can say, "Been there, done that." Instead of a tender conversation with the Lord, prayer that satisfies itself simply with the attainment of a psychic state or psychological achievement, no matter how enlightening, can easily become a meaningless monologue that never connects with anything beyond the most exterior abodes of created existence.

Avoiding Extreme Individualism

In our own day, one Camaldolese hermit describes the dominance in extreme individualism among those pursuing the spiritual life. He believes that the contemporary presumption that the world is only an appearance has impacted the way we approach prayer. We conflate our ego with the mystery of God and make ourselves vulnerable to all kinds of magical thinking, "If the supreme criterion of life in Christ is no longer adherence in faith to the Triune God, but personal experience, the change to a religious syncretism will be quickly made."[45]

In fact, many Catholics are drawn to syncretism. A form of magical thinking, it blends practices from different religious traditions, Christian and non-Christian. It claims to transcend religious differences by taking what is deemed good about each one. Like the teaching of some of the Beatas of Saint Teresa's

---

[45] In Praise of Hiddenness: The Spirituality of the Camaldolese Hermits of Monte Corona (Bloomingdale, OH: Ercam Editions, 2007), 53.

time, our contemporary syncretism proposes a Jesus without the Church, a spiritual experience without a creed, and a spirituality without religion.

When judgment about what is true is based solely on someone's subjective spiritual experience, the possibility for confusion and deception are great. In other words, magical thinking is vulnerable to the unchallenged personal biases and assumptions. Esoteric claims can have unresolved and dangerous incoherences. One's personal integrity and one's ability to connect with others in truth is diminished. Sooner or later, even mutually agreed-upon fantasies fail to provide solid enough footing for genuine encounters with God and with one another.

It is pathetic to presume that the Almighty fits into whatever appeals to the latest religious fantasy. When we allow ourselves to be limited by the religious products of our time, we are unable to get beyond ourselves. Because of our propensity to self-deception, this is dangerous ground and cannot uphold the weight of our existence.

On a deeper level, we must wonder whether behind all this spiritual consumerism there might lurk some unchecked aggression toward God. We are not benignly indifferent to the Father's love for us. As we descend into the depths of our being, we discover nasty strongholds of sinful resistance to His love.

Compounding the problem of magical thinking is a naïveté concerning the claims of psychology. Instead of going into deep prayer, searching the Scriptures, and pondering the wisdom of the saints, many professional spiritual masters advocate psychological self-help techniques. Psychology might help us manage some elements of this aggression to some degree. This science has made important progress in providing remedies for many affective and cognitive pathologies and disorders. But there are many wounds it cannot heal. Products and programs of mere human cleverness cannot vanquish the ancient hostility that threatens our humanity.

Confronting Hostility to God

Hostility to God is a vicious absence of a love that ought to be, but is not. When Saint Paul calls this "the flesh," he is not referring to something inherent to our physical or bodily existence. Instead, he adamantly affirms the resurrection of the body throughout his works. It is a power that opposes our spiritual life: inclining us to fail to do the good we intend to and to do evil things we do not intend to (see Rom. 7:15).

If harmony in our lives is characterized by how we love, this lack of love is a disease that disorders our relationship to ourselves, to others, and to God. Any lack of love in us is a malignant spiritual cancer that, if unchecked, will kill us. It is a misery that only God's mercy can heal.

The answer to this hostility is the practice of mental prayer rooted in the teachings of the Church. An authentically Christian conversation with God about the whole of one's life during periods of silence has had unmatched success for Christians throughout the centuries. In grace-filled contemplation, the world is not an appearance but the place God manifests His glory.

Christians turn to prayer and commit themselves to a conversatio morum precisely because the self is not God but someone in whom God has placed His hope. Prostrating ourselves before the One who is so beautifully other than we are — this is our freedom from individualism and self-centeredness. A true dialogue with our crucified God humbly discovers a way to accept all of life, even the most painful parts, as a remarkable gift.

9

HOPE AND COMPUNCTION

Christian hope requires a deep attentiveness to the Lord, a receptivity of heart that goes beyond the simple fulfillment of a religious obligation. By faith, we already possess the substance of our hope. Prayer searches reasons for our hope given to us in the truths of our faith.

To achieve this prayer needs constancy, determination, and perseverance. Without such devotion, we are not receptive enough to find a reason for the hope we have inside. Not only does this make it difficult to witness to others, but our own life of faith is put at risk.

Many people who serve God complain that they do not pray because they do not have time. They have so many responsibilities to fulfill that there is no time left for prayer. In fact, they highly suspect prayer to be a waste of time or even a kind of indulgent behavior.

Of course, they do what they are supposed to do and say those prayers out loud that everyone expects them to pray. They do not, however, consistently invest their hearts in prayer—at least not fully. Behind this approach to the spiritual life lurks the presumption that, all things being equal, I am "good enough." And behind this presumption is the deeper suspicion that at the end of the day, God is not really there for me.

Anyone who feels this way almost always thinks that such doubts are not really dealt with in Christianity—that a real Christian could not possibly have to deal with this question. Because such a believer is ashamed or embarrassed by this concern, because this disciple does not share it with anyone but tries to deal with it on his own, this unfaced challenge to prayer undermines his piety in a very practical and intimate way, even to the point of making of his whole spirituality an empty show.

Many discouraged disciples, rather than really entering into a conversation with the Lord and those He sends to them wind up trying to do everything on their own. They either end in total failure or merely muddle through, day after day. Barely managing life's many challenges—they have learned to exist, perhaps even somewhat successfully, but they have not learned to live life to the full.

Some cynically conclude that this is how all Christians, all people of faith are doing it—that no one with brains actually believes or prays at all. Thus, we live at a time when many of us who say that we are Christians do not really pray as Christians should. We do not live our faith, we do not ask God, and we do not seek the counsel of those who know Him. We are left on our own, wondering why we are disconnected from ourselves, from others, and from God.

This kind of faith without real prayer is not real faith. This kind of life is only halfway. We are not "good enough" by ourselves. Without God, the little goodness that is ours can quickly be lost. Only He can bring to fullness the goodness that He first has given us. Without really praying to Him from the depths of our hearts, we have not allowed Him to give us the fullness of life He yearns for us to know.

Prayer and Ongoing Conversion

Teresa de Ahumada's prayer was a partial and sporadic conversation with the Lord until she had a deeper encounter with Him. Teresa was born in 1515 into a pious family. Her mother died when she was only thirteen. At the age of twenty, against her father's will, she sneaked off to become a Carmelite nun. Although she lived a disciplined and pious life, especially by contemporary standards, her deeper conversion happened almost twenty years later.

By the time she was in her late thirties, Sister Teresa felt her external practices had become little more than an empty show. In her heart, she was holding back from the Lord. Afraid to trust Him, she could not find the deeper faith that she needed really to pray. She was unhappy with herself but felt unable to do anything about it.

Teresa of Ávila knew, deep inside, that she was not "good enough." She carried a sense of guilt that she had not been as generous with God as she ought to be. She did not know, however, how she could trust God. Every time she began to become fervent in devotion, something would happen to pull her back. Constant backsliding robbed her of hope. She wrestled with the idea that the Lord was disappointed and perhaps even angry with her. Her life had become a charade, and she did not know how to recover her integrity. How can anyone cast concerns on the Lord if she does not really believe that He is actually concerned for her?

We are not meant to muddle through life without God. He has planned out our lives so that we will learn to look to Him in prayer. He is a merciful Father whose deepest stance toward us is not disappointment or anger, but love. In fact, He waits for us, pierced to the heart over everything we have suffered. Finding Him is to find the fullness of life itself.

Just as we are inclined to do, Teresa learned the rituals of a pious life until her mastery of them impressed almost everyone around her. She even pretended to pray, and in pretending she soon began to lose altogether her ability to pray. Her natural charm and wit hid from all but those who most loved her the spiritual incoherence that haunted her soul. Living by the pretext of prayer allowed her to maintain her reputation, but it was not ultimately satisfying. Anyone who knows this experience knows that she ventured into one of the most disconcerting doctrines of Christian piety.

There is real peril without real prayer. Without prayer our integrity, our authenticity with others, our connection with God are all at grave risk. Indifference to Christ on a practical and lived level begins to grow—and so does our indifference to everyone entrusted to us. Until prayer becomes a real effort *actually* to listen to the Lord, losing one's faith altogether remains a real possibility.

For Teresa of Ávila, an unexpected grace changed all this. She learned to listen first of all not by discovering a new technique or mastering a new spiritual practice. Instead, it was a wholly simple moment of her heart: a movement of belief, of hope, and of love.

On her way to liturgy with her community, Teresa of Ávila glanced at a statue of Christ. This image depicted Him after the scourging, crowned with thorns, the *Man of Sorrows* (Isa. 53:3). The purpose of this kind of sacred art is to put us in the moment, to help us remember what the Lord has done for us. This is what happened to Teresa.

Her eyes met His. In this instant, she was no longer simply gazing on a statue. In a moment that seemed to be outside of time, she experienced the Lord Himself looking at her with love. He who was wounded for her sake now gazed at her, personally, with tender love and deep compassion. In this gaze, she saw herself and her lack of devotion in a whole new way.

This loving presence of the Lord was so intense, the Mother of the Carmelite Reform in Spain and future Doctor of the Church, knelt down in tears. She begged the Lord for the grace not to backslide again, and she did not rise until she was convinced that the Lord had given her this grace.[46] Such tears always pierce the heart of God, and Teresa was humbled by the humiliated love of Christ.

Compunction and Devotion in Prayer

It is said that after his conversion, Saint Ignatius could not stop weeping. He shed tears all the time. This is so much the case that only through the gift of tears do we really understand the spiritual exercises that he proposed. Saint Teresa of Ávila also recommends this way of tears. In them is found a mysterious consolation that only God's presence can give.

For great mystics like Saint Teresa of Ávila or Saint Ignatius of Loyola, the heart-piercing awareness of the Lord's presence that they sought by faith often caused them to weep—both exteriorly and interiorly. Prayer rooted in conversatio morum is always open to these tears. In their case, this holy sorrow helped them pray and to grow in virtue because it is a sorrow informed by love and gratitude.

Pondering Christ's Incarnation and work of redemption against her own indifference, Saint Teresa would wash her

---

[46] She relates this story herself in *The Book of Her Life*, chap. 9, in *The Collected Works of St. Teresa of Ávila*, vol. 1, trans. Kieran Kavanaugh, O.C.D., and Otilio Rodriguez, O.C.D. (Washington, DC: ICS, 2002), 100–104.

memory with hope. As she learned to invoke the Holy Spirit in the midst of difficult spiritual struggles, her heart was pierced by love, and she was freed from attachments that held her back. At the end of each day, she would spend an hour weeping with Jesus in the Agony of the Garden before falling asleep.

The most difficult obstacle to this kind of prayer is our own distracted minds. We have filled our imagination with impure images, and we have entertained whole ways of thinking that are opposed to the tenderness that deep prayer requires. A kind of sluggish indifference can pull at us when we try to pray. At the same time, if we make the decision to turn our attention to holy things with love, God's gentle power is brought to bear in surprising ways. All it takes on our part is determination and perseverance in prayer.

When the thought of Christ evokes tears, whether physical or spiritual, the virtues of our spiritual life grow. Tears of compunction are like water for the garden of our heart. Compunction, in fact, means to be pierced to the heart. These tears, whether physical or spiritual, make the virtues of our spiritual life grow and flourish. Teresa of Ávila described this kind of devotion as water for the flower garden of our hearts, the place where Christian virtues are meant to flourish.

Devotion is not the external fulfillment of religious obligations. One can be self-consciously devout in appearance but lack devotion of heart. Looking and sounding spiritual is easy. *Being* spiritual requires the hard work of actual and ongoing surrender of one's heart to God. In fact, it is possible to be very observant of one's religious obligations but not actually be devout at all.

Devotion is commitment to be sincere and vulnerable to God interiorly, in season and out of season. It cannot be seen or measured from the outside, but everyone is drawn to its sincerity and attracted by its integrity. Without this decision of the heart for the Lord, our religious observances can easily become blasphemous acts of self-delusion. With this interior disposition, one possesses a powerful tool to combat hypocrisy and backsliding.

This dedication of heart chooses the Lord as the ultimate priority of one's life under which every other priority and concern must fall. This choice is not on the level of wishful thinking or vague intention. It plays out in an immediate readiness to respond completely and hold nothing back.

Devotion has this note of immediate generosity because it is immediately aware of how devoted the Lord is to each one of us. It does not try to prove itself or gain divine approval. It has, instead, the character of tender mutuality between God and the soul. Beholding the intensity of God's love, the attentiveness of devotion yearns to provide some token of gratitude in the here and now.

10

LOVE AND OBEDIENCE

We have been exploring how the commitment to conversatio morum found in the rule of Saint Benedict opens up one's whole existence to fire from above. This conversation with the Lord and conversion of life personally implicates us in the teachings of the Church and to a personal encounter with the Lord that is ongoing. This kind of conversation with God involves, as Teresa of Ávila witnesses, a life of conversion, a reorientation of our lives, and the constant effort to stay on course. In this way, conversatio morum is a lifelong journey, a pilgrimage of faith into the service of the Lord.

Because we are inclined to disobedience, readiness to repent, to do penance, and to rededicate ourselves to the Lord is a necessary part of this journey. The English verb *repent* comes from the Latin *re-pentare*, to rethink or to think in a new way. We are able to repent and change our course because learning to listen and respond to the Lord allows us to be open to His blessings. Because He wants to bless us abundantly, the Lord is constantly at work disclosing Himself in new and unfamiliar ways to strengthen and deepen our loving obedience to Him.

When we are disobedient in even the smallest things, He challenges us to change course in order to help us. Whenever His truth pierces us to the heart, He is guiding us away from the unhappiness that currently threatens our existence. At the same time, our contrite hearts are made more ready for the fullness that He longs for us to know.

The obedience of love is made perfect through suffering and trials. There are irrational currents below the surface of our humanity and overwhelming storms above it. God permits these evils because the possibility of human freedom and friendship cannot exist without them. Whether unconscious or subliminal, whether originating because of our failures or the sins of others against us, the Lord uses these life ambiguities to make our obedience and love for Him and one another beautiful and pure.

Contemplative prayer in the face of trial is oriented to this work God is accomplishing in us. In particular, the wisdom to discern how best to serve the Lord in the face of inadequacy or failure helps us sanctify these necessary ambiguities. We can do this no matter what we have done or what others have done to us because God is always acting with even greater industry and power to bring all things under the Lordship of Christ. It is possible to base one's life on what He is doing, to root ourselves in His saving work. Through vigilant discernment of what the Lord is bringing to perfection in our life and in the world, we can find and embrace the most appropriate way to serve Him.

This kind of prayer requires regular periods of silent listening in our hearts to the Word made flesh. When trials come, we need to make every effort to pray even more. We cannot discern what the Risen Lord is saying to us about our lives and motives if we do not spend time attending to Him. If we are attentive, His voice becomes the beacon by which we find our way out of a jungle of guilt and into the friendship for which we were made.

The Silence of God

There are many good Catholics who claim they do not hear the voice of God. When they pray, they describe a silent emptiness. They are concerned that their effort to pray is a waste of time; they are not convinced that the Lord speaks to them.

The language of the Lord, however, is mysterious. One could say that He speaks by silences. His silence is not empty but is filled with meaning for the heart that searches it in faith. He speaks His Word in silence. This divine silence in which the Word is entrusted to us silences the unspoken self-absorption that rants against prayer. We can attend to this silent fullness only by faith.

The silence of our misery envelops the last cry of the Word made flesh in death and, at the same time, our misery is enveloped by the new life this cry won for us. We humbly embrace this heartrending silence by choosing to believe in the love that is disclosed in it. Especially when we can find no reason to do so, something powerful is being shared with us from above.

In the obedience of our faith, the silent misery of our lives is baptized in the silence of God's love. Jesus' obedience embraced even the silence after His last wordless cry and filled that silence with meaning. Christian obedience in prayer explores this holy silence too.

Our conversation with the Lord draws us into this silent stillness. This is not a silence beyond obedience or doctrine or meaning. Instead, it leads to even-deeper abodes of obedient love, a silence that rests in the deep things of God to which the whole teaching of the Church is ordered. Contemplative prayer takes us to the threshold of this sanctuary, where gifts between God and man are exchanged.

In extreme circumstances and bitter duress, humble silence before the Lord can be an act of faith, the effort to believe that

He is love and that He has not abandoned us. This obedience is tested and purified when He seems silent and absent from our lives. To believe in love and to choose to love because of the love Christ revealed—this deep moment in our conversation is beyond words. In this attentiveness to love and its strange silence, a mysterious space is expanded in the very depths of our existence and our lives are intensified in ways we do not understand.

The more we go down this hidden pathway of obedience, the more we learn to think like Christ. Some of our pursuits that we believed to be so important now seem silly and a waste of time. Bad habits such as petty bickering or careless irreverence suddenly take on new proportions. At one moment we did not think these things to be so bad; now, in the silence of God's love, they are revealed as an egregious offense against His holiness.

The Witness of Faustina Kowalska

To help us see this powerful connection between obedience and love in our conversation with God, we conclude this chapter with the spiritual experiences of Saint Faustina Kowalska.

Before she had made the decision to enter religious life, Helen Kowalska was trying unsuccessfully to have a good time with her friends and other young adults in the area. She was at a dance—a wonderful opportunity to meet other young people. Yet, her heart was not in it, and she felt that she ought to be somewhere else.

A couple of years before, she told her parents that she wanted to enter religious life. They forbade her to do so and sent her to get a job instead. She did not question this and did what they asked. She was now working as a housekeeper, trying to fit in with everybody else. But she was not happy.

Just as the dance was to start, she saw Jesus standing on the dance floor before her. This was the suffering and humiliated

Christ who gazed into her eyes. He asked her, "How long will you keep putting me off?"[47]

In a single moment, Helen Kowalska was pierced to the heart. She repented over not having made more of an effort to follow through with her desire for religious life a few years before. She was also convinced in a new way that the Lord had a special plan for her and that she needed to trust in what He desired for her life.

Now, in this moment, she knew that she had to respond. Her life, going in one way, suddenly took a turn for another. She quietly left the dance and ran to a church to listen to the Lord.

This immediate response of faith and the turning around of her life are both characteristic of a real encounter with the Lord. Prayer begins at God's initiative, but He also expects us to respond. When we respond, we open ourselves even more to the wonderful gifts that He yearns to give.

While she was in prayer, before the Eucharistic presence of the Lord, Faustina felt the Lord call her to go by train, miles away, to Warsaw. When she arrived, she would enter the first convent that would accept her.

She knew that this would be a radical and inconvenient move. The experience of God's thirst in our lives is never convenient or comfortable and always takes us into situations that are difficult and unfamiliar. Her heart was convinced that this was an invitation from the Lord.

Like Abraham, she obeyed. After settling her affairs and explaining to her sister what had happened, she went to Warsaw. Without knowing exactly which convent she was to enter, she

---

[47] Saint Maria Faustina Kowalska, *Diary: Divine Mercy in My Soul* (Stockbridge, MA: Marian Press, 2008), 7.

was resolved to be generously available to whatever the Lord would lead her to.

This began a great pattern in her life and prayer. Christ would ask her to do things; and as she learned to obey Him, their conversation together would deepen and open new mysteries. Through this kind of prayer, she learned to trust Jesus, who filled her life with deep meaning and joy, hidden in suffering and the misunderstanding of others.

She would live for only another thirteen years, and for most of these, she was profoundly misunderstood and thought to be delusional. Yet the message of God's mercy she experienced and promoted sustained many Catholics during and after the apocalyptic events of World War II. Canonized by Pope Saint John Paul II, Faustina Kowalska would become among the most influential saints of the twentieth century. Her insights into the Lord's thirst help us understand His expectations concerning our prayer:

> I wait for souls, and they are indifferent toward Me. I love them tenderly and sincerely, and they distrust Me. I want to lavish My graces on them and they do not want to accept them. They treat me as a dead object.[48]

Christian prayer and the obedience it requires are extremely interpersonal, an I-thou relationship, a mutual and tender heart-to-heart. It proposes that God is really real, a Someone who wants us to know Him personally. As such, God is not indifferent to our attitudes toward Him and He has expectations of us. The obedience He seeks is that of a heart that burns for love of Him in the same way that He loves, a love that is grateful for all, that surrenders all, that gives all.

[48] Ibid., 511.

II

THE BATTLE FOR PEACE

"Peace depends on victory, and victory depends on struggle. If you desire peace, you will struggle continuously.

"Your 'weapons' in this struggle are meditation, self-denial, the sacraments, the rosary, and recollection. Your allies are Mary, Joseph, the angels, your patron saints, and your spiritual director. Unless you gradually drop your weapons or betray your allies, your victory is assured."[49]

Archbishop Nguyen Van Thuan wrote these words on the back of a calendar and entrusted them to a young boy. He was in prison, and he knew the faithful of his archdiocese needed encouragement. After years of war, defeat, and humiliation, many of them were losing hope. The struggle to pray and be devoted to their faith seemed meaningless. The archbishop knew from his experience in prison that continuous struggle against sin through faithfulness to prayer was the only path to true peace. This was the message that he was smuggling out of the Communist reeducation camp. It was a word of hope.

---

[49] Francis Xavier Cardinal Nguyen Van Thuan, *The Road to Hope: A Gospel from Prison*, trans. Peter Bookallil (Boston: Pauline Books and Media, 2001), 17.

The Archbishop of Saigon turned prisons in Vietnam into places of hope not only for his fellow prisoners but also for his guards. It was a decision he made when he was first incarcerated. At the time, he complained to the Lord in prayer. All his plans and important works were at risk because the Lord had allowed him to be imprisoned. As he complained, the Lord helped him see that anxiously tormenting himself with this kind of prayer was not a way forward. He needed to let go of his plans and the way he thought it should be.

The Lord was inviting him to surrender completely to the divine plan and this meant entering into a struggle. All he had was the present moment, and he needed to do everything within his power to live it with as much love as possible. Living the present moment with love made space for God to work. To live like this is to realize the victory of good over evil. This struggle to love through prayer was the path to peace.

The Communists tried to break him by torturing and tormenting him. He endured nine years of solitary confinement in his thirteen years of prison. Humiliated, mocked, threatened, beaten—sometimes it was difficult for him to utter even simple vocal prayers. Yet even when he was completely overcome emotionally, mentally, and physically, he did not lose hope.

In the most difficult situations, Christ crucified gave him all he needed, and the archbishop learned to rely on Him alone. He kept extending the hand of forgiveness and friendship to his tormentors. He never failed to find ways to encourage his fellow inmates.

By keeping his eyes on the Lord, the archbishop understood that he was on a journey even in prison. Not by worrying about the future or tormenting himself with missed opportunities, but by putting as much love in the present moment as he could, he was making that moment into another step toward his goal. The trail he was blazing was a road to hope: "If the cross is the standard by which you make your choices and decisions, your soul will be at peace."[50]

The Way of the Cross

After God awakens us spiritually and we set out on a pilgrimage through the darkness of our hearts to find Him, we soon discover that this quest is being taken up in the midst of a great spiritual war. Unlike a platonic worldview, in which the higher realms of spiritual existence are more peaceful than the lower worlds of material being, our apostolic faith reveals that there is war in heaven, and the earth is an enemy-occupied battlefield.[51] The enemies we confront in this war are not distractions from our goal — even when they are distracting! God has put everything in our life to help us make progress. God uses even these spiritual enemies who stand in our way to make our love stronger and more real.

The battle for the heart is waged in the mind, or so the Desert Fathers taught. Seeking the truth about God is the only way to realize the victory He won for us. Although the victory of good over evil is already won, this victory can be realized on a personal level in each individual heart only through the grace of God. The decision of the heart to cling to God requires a loving knowledge of the truth. As long as we allow our lives to

---

[50] Nguyen Van Thuan, *The Road of Hope: A Gospel from Prison*, trans. Peter Bookallil, Boston: Pauline Books and Media (2001) 227.

[51] See for example Revelation 12:7–12 and Ephesians 6:11–18. St. Athanasius presents the ascetic as a champion in this battle, see his *Life of Antony*.

be guided by fantasy or inordinate desires, the heart is robbed of the truth it needs to choose the good and avoid evil.

Sometimes we do not pray because the truth of prayer has been obscured. It appears an irrational waste of time in an exponentially accelerating world. In a culture in which value is assigned either by productivity or entertainment, prayer appears out of place for it does not seem to produce very many immediate tangible results. True prayer is nonetheless neither an inefficient use of time nor an entertaining diversion from what is really important.

True prayer is about dealing with the truth about God and ourselves. Truth gives God the space He needs to act in our lives and in situations. This means that prayer is about accepting responsibility for our actions but trusting in Divine Mercy even more. Prayer sometimes means renouncing anxiety over circumstances we cannot control and instead choosing to trust in divine providence in the face of catastrophe. Prayer is about finding a word of hope that we can share with others even when we are too exhausted and overwhelmed to feel very hopeful ourselves. We fight for the truth by prayer so that we might live by the truth in our actions and in the way we deal with one another.

We need prayer, not because of anything it produces, but most of all because it is good for us to humble ourselves before God, to realize how much we need Him, and to acknowledge His goodness. When prayer is rooted in truth, it opens us to this beautiful knowledge of the heart, a loving knowledge that fills life with meaning. This wisdom for life is why doctrine and prayer must be brought together into an encounter with Christ.

We fight a battle for the truth because only when we meet the Lord do our lives really change. Contemplation of God and knowing the truth about ourselves go hand in hand. When these are joined in the effort to pray, a new power is unleashed, and this fire from heaven transforms not only one's own life, but the whole world.

Christ Brings Peace into our Human Situations

Earlier in this work we have already considered how Jesus speaks to the whole person, from the deepest primal urges to the loftiest powers of speculation. Nothing human is outside the scope of His dynamic truth. He is the truth that unfolds in a place deeper than conscious, unconscious, or even subliminal thought, feeling, imagination, memory, or intuition. We identified this place of encounter as the heart.

In the battle for peace, our faith claims that the Risen Lord is able to speak into the human situation, its depths and heights, because He has, Himself, a human heart united in His own person to His divinity. From this heart, which our sins pierced open, He reigns in the spiritual center of every heart. In this human being for others, He knows where the tragic depths and heights and horizons of humanity coincide, and He brings into our misery His mercy.

In Him, God fills the voids and inadequacies, the hopes and the joys, the anxieties and sorrows of being human in this world below with wisdom from above. He is able to bring us this peace because He understands us and is connected to us—not only humanity in general, but each of us in particular, because He has made our humanity His own. Far from rejecting or condemning the ambiguities and brokenness of those who call to Him, He longs to heal each one and restore that person's dignity. He knows how to lead souls out of their alienation and draw them into the communion that He enjoys with the Father. Christian contemplation allows Him to establish the soul in this great stillness of Divine Love and communicate His whole saving mystery to this end.

God's fullness and human emptiness: the collision of these opposing forces in the heart is mortally dangerous. Yet God has risked this because what is at stake is important to Him and so very wonderful for us. The hidden mystery of future glory puts a limit on the present suffering and evil into which the encounter baptizes both God and man. If we give God our confidence, He will see us through this great trial.

The Lord does not want this moment to destroy us, but He also yearns for our friendship, and He knows without this difficult moment, we will never find the ground on which a true friendship can find its footing. Unless we embrace this moment of truth with Him, our hostility thwarts the desire of His Heart. This is why He chose to die for us: so that we might live for this moment. By allowing the unholy fury of our hearts to spend itself against His ardent desire for our love, He found the pathway by which He could descend into the depths of our misery and on this pathway, we find the gateway to mercy.

Approaching Divine Judgment

To pray is to face the hour of judgment. Just as at our death we will come before the Judge of Heaven and Earth to give an accounting of ourselves, all real prayer also starts before this same tribunal. To submit freely to the justice of God brings us into contact with His merciful love. There is nothing that we have done that He will not forgive—if we humbly ask Him with a contrite heart.

God judges from a throne of power and wisdom—but this throne is too great to be limited to any physical or visible space. It is wherever God is. Because Christians have received the indwelling of the Holy Trinity through the gift of the Holy Spirit at Baptism, the soul is a temple, a dwelling place for God in the fullness of His glory.

Our conscience is transformed by the divine indwelling. It is not alienated in its own ignorance, but instead is implicated in God's indwelling presence. It is subject to all the divine majesty and awe of heaven, even if it experiences these realities only in the obscurity of faith. This is why the throne of grace from which the Lord reigns in heaven can be found when we enter within and prayerfully attend to our own conscience. This voice is meant to mediate the law that the Creator has written in our nature. If we allow this voice to be formed by our faith, the Almighty can even use it to reveal heaven's judgments on our actions and where we stand before Him.

This means that the Holy Spirit can be speaking to us through our conscience. He may move our conscience to warn us or admonish us or confirm us in our actions. Yet this is true only insofar as we have formed our consciences in the truth. Our consciences are like a sacrament—the voice of conscience is a sign of the voice of the Holy Spirit in us.

At the same time, our own ignorance can limit the ways in which God desires to communicate to us. Our consciences are not infallible. Often, they are not meant to be the only thing we rely on in a moral judgment. Against the many difficult moral complexities of modern life, we need good catechesis, the counsel of others, and time in moral discernment.

This is where prayer in moral discernment is so important. Prayer listens to the voice of conscience to discover and obey the voice of God. It submits our conscience to the rule of faith so that it can discover the most appropriate ways to serve the Lord in the midst of the ambiguities of life. Prayer opens us to the promptings of the Holy Spirit—who may move us with the gifts of counsel and knowledge in ways that go beyond the calculations of unaided wisdom.

This kind of openness in prayer, however, requires a humble and contrite spirit. Whenever we willingly confess our sins with the intention of changing our lives, God's mercy is always there for us. How we humble ourselves before the judgment seat of God in prayer is practice for how we will come before Him when we await His final judgment. When we approach Him pierced to the heart for what He has done for us, we have already embraced an eschatological conversion, a rethinking of how we conduct ourselves before the gaze of our heavenly Father.

When we take up prayer to answer the vexing riddle of our lives, we are making a decision to submit ourselves to the judgment of the Lord. Freely to lay ourselves bare before the Lord is a solemn moment of vulnerability and truth before God. In this spiritual nakedness by which we examine ourselves from the Lord's perspective, we also begin to see just how vulnerable God has made Himself for us. However deep we contemplate the misery that we bear and that we have caused, there is a deeper insight into the immensity of His mercy waiting to be discovered. The treasury of His love is inexhaustible.

Spiritual exercises will help with this effort, but only so far. He discloses his love in the silent fullness of His Word. It is a heart-to-heart, a conversation of truth—the truth about the lack of truth in our hearts and the truth about His love suffering this lack for our sake. At certain moments, our efforts concede to His. The sheer majesty of His love surrounds us in holiness even if we do not feel it and think we are wasting our time.

There is a moment in which we must throw down our crowns and let go of all attempts at self-justification. In authentic

Christian prayer, every ideological head must bow, every cause-driven knee must bend, and every social agenda–spun tongue must declare that Jesus Christ is Lord. Our own agenda may well have a good justification, but that justification is always subordinate to His justice. We must dispossess ourselves of self-righteous and arrogant attitudes. Purity and humility are the only worthy clothing in His presence.

Techniques, methods, and forms of piety are secondary to being in right relationship with the Lord. We do not approach Him to gain a new experience or to acquire a new state of consciousness. No mercenary attitude toward the things of God can take us very far into the depths of His mystery.

This does not mean that various kinds of vocal prayer or ways of meditation are not helpful. It is just that reading the Bible, praying the Rosary, or entering into silence are all subordinate to being reconciled with God and cleaving to Him by faith. We can perform all these pious acts, but without love and humble faith they are meaningless clanging in the presence of the Almighty.

There is something in us that is hostile to God. Have you ever noticed after being invited to visit a nursing home or pray the Stations of the Cross or do some other good work that, instead of being grateful for the opportunity, there is a certain aversion, even a peculiar dread that takes hold? Even if we suffer this feeling only momentarily, this is a real glimpse of the hostility to God raging within us.

We resist many gentle promptings to pray because we tend to see our Creator in opposition to us. What we want conflicts with what the Lord demands. Religion, piety, holiness seem like burdens that weigh down our spirit. We want our freedom, and the Lord, with His moral demands, seems to want to take it away. We want to be in control of our own destiny, and He demands that we submit our lives to Him instead. Our free will and His divine will seem mutually exclusive.

Fighting this spiritual resistance in us is the battle for peace that we must find in our souls. God has given us the gift of who we are—and He expects us to rise to the challenge, to win the victory that will establish peace. It is a struggle with pride and hubris, with despair and slothfulness, with greed and anger. We cannot win this struggle on our own, but if we do not forsake our friends and do not drop our weapons, Christ Himself will come to help us. He comes with fire from above—and sets all our efforts ablaze with His love.

The Greatness of Christian Prayer for Humanity

The apostle Paul exclaims that the mystery of Christian piety is great. The discipline of the Lord entails a filial piety that begins and ends with prayer. Christ's confident and humble cry to the Father reveals His deepest desires, and only those who enter into His prayer really come to understand His heart.

In Christian piety, the mystery of devotion and our efforts at beginning to pray are about entering ever more deeply into the heart of Christ. From His heart, an endless sea of the deepest desires flow, desires that resonate with the will of the Father. The most intimate of these was offered the night before He died:

Father, I desire that they also, whom thou hast given me, may be with me where I am, to behold my glory which thou hast given me in thy love for me before the foundation of the world. (John 17:24)[52]

[52] Saint Paul sheds light on this prayer of Jesus in 2 Corinthians 3:18.

This prayer of Jesus, uttered with full knowledge of His impending Passion and death, assumes we understand what glory the Father gave and continues to give to Jesus. Glory is the radiance of personal greatness, and true glory is almost always hidden in this world. The one who sees someone in his glory really knows the truth about that person. To see the glory of the Lord is to know Who He is.

Toward a New Culture of Life

Such a life is ordered to a new kind of society, an authentic communion and friendship with God and with one another. Whenever this new life begins again, Jesus' prayer "that they may be one" is realized (John 17:11). The glory of the Cross is revealed.

The world is being ordered for a new kind of society, and this society is being realized all the time. The Risen Lord is in communion with the Father, in a forever new society of profound joy and love, a fellowship entered into not only at the end of life, but right now in prayer. Prayer allows this society to break into this world, establishing a culture of life and giving birth to a civilization of love.

The Church in Korea is very young and has been very persecuted. Saint John Paul II calls the northern region "the Church of Silence." This present oppression in the North, however, does not seem substantially different from policies enacted against Christians by other Korean governments in the last two hundred years. History suggests that the more governments oppress the faithful of Korea, the stronger their faith becomes. Their example helps us understand that in the midst of severe circumstances, the greatness of Christian piety calls us to redouble the practices of the faith.

FIRE FROM ABOVE

The Christian faith began to spread throughout Korea about the same time as Saint Junípero Serra was founding the California Missions. After a small group of scholars brought it from China, it quickly spread among the common people. Especially those who were marginalized on the peripheries of Korean society found hope in the wisdom this new religion offered, and this hope gave them a new sense of dignity and solidarity with one another.

As is the case now in the northern part of the Korean peninsula, the determination and spiritual strength of this solidarity was severely tested. Those in power felt that this new religion was subversive to Korean society because it seemed to encourage friendships and marriages across economic and social classes. Not unlike pagan Rome, the aristocracy believed Christians were not loyal to Korean social values. To preserve better social order, violent persecutions were undertaken throughout the nineteenth century, and this resulted in the martyrdom of over ten thousand Christians.

One of these believers was Saint Thomas Son Chason. After his bishop was imprisoned, he went to claim Church property the government had confiscated. He did so at the invitation of the government officials who had taken them. It was, of course, a trap. He was imprisoned after a brief interview. In an effort to get him to renounce his faith, he was tortured and tormented for months. The more he was pressed, the more he rigorously observed the pious practices of his faith.

For him and for the other Korean martyrs, faithfulness to his baptismal promises was more important than life itself. He rooted himself in prayer and interpreted his suffering as a way to thank Christ for suffering for his salvation. He not only fasted from food (it was Lent), but he also exercised patience under great physical and psychological duress and found the strength to bear his circumstances with extraordinary dignity. He witnessed to his faith whenever he was being coerced or manipulated to reject it. This proved to be a testimony not only to those who were being persecuted with him but also to those who persecuted him.

His persecutors were astonished and frustrated that, even under these circumstances, they could not overcome his devotion or his bold speech about the faith. Before he was strangled to death by his tormentors, he confessed that although his wounds were painful, he also believed that he experienced the healing touch of Jesus and Mary in them. He was winning the battle for peace even though he looked defeated in every other way.[53]

Today, despite ongoing efforts like these, the Church in Korea is growing and continues to be a transforming presence for Korean society. It is a thriving Church whether confronting the unbridled materialism of the South or the religious hatred of the North. Hostility to God has a limit, but His love is limitless, and at the end of the day the victory of good over evil will be known by all Koreans because of this wisdom from above.

Prayer, because it makes space for God to order the world so that humanity might thrive to the full, is thus, fundamentally, an act of grace-imbued intelligence. Once we understand that prayer involves supernatural rationality, the nature of things opposed to prayer becomes clear. All forms of irrationality stand as the adversaries to prayer. Prayer grows in freedom and truth the more it confronts and overcomes irrationality. Yet the forms

---

[53] See Charles Dallet, *Histoire de L'Église de Corée* (Paris: Victor Palmé, 1874), 2:560–561.

of irrationality are more vast, ancient, and clever than human intelligence can cope with alone. In order for prayer to mature, it must take up a spiritual battle against these forces, and it must do so wrapped in faith and completely reliant on God.

12

CROSSING THE FRONTIER

The Christian tradition knows three principal enemies of prayer: the world, the flesh, and the devil. Saint John of the Cross describes these as wild animals, frontiers, and thugs.[54] In order to progress on our journey into intimacy with Christ we must confront the world, all kinds of irrational powers, and even our own hostility to the Lord.

In *Hidden Mountain, Secret Garden*, I provided brief reflections on all three of these enemies of prayer. This is because we were looking at the whole journey of prayer more in general. This present work focuses on mystical wisdom. In regard to this wisdom, the greatest enemy that needs to be confronted is our own wounded humanity.

Mystical wisdom can unfold in the heart only when it is supernaturally secure with itself. Without a prayerful sense of self-possession, our possession of wisdom is only precarious. Conversely, ignorance of one's own dignity and lack of acceptance

---

[54] See his commentary *Spiritual Canticle* 3:1–10. *Thugs* may not precisely translate the term used by the Carmelite master. However, translating *los fuertes* as merely "strong men" sounds too benign for the trouble irrational forces cause the spiritual life. Ruffians, brutes, or bullies would be closer to what he describes. This text will refer to *los fuertes* as *thugs*.

or of what it means to be a man or a woman is dangerous to our integrity. So, rather than going over all the material previously presented, we will focus on the importance of dealing with this particular enemy of prayer—an enemy that can become our closest friend.

Crossing the frontiers is not a matter of surmounting our humanity to grasp an abstract absolute. Nor is it a simple traversing from self-understanding into self-nihilism. It is departing from concerns that belong to the periphery of human existence so that we can arrive at what is at the center of our existence.

In itself, human nature is a pathway to the Lord. Each person and our solidarity together are fashioned as a living icon of God: three in one and one in three. An icon is above all a window through which heaven gazes on us. Through our humanity as individuals in communion with one another and for one another, God gazes on the world.

We start this journey quite outside ourselves. We do not begin with anything but the faintest awareness of the One in whose image we have been fashioned. Neither do we live out of any real awareness that we bear His likeness. Instead, we are preoccupied with many superficial concerns at the peripheries of our existence. As we progress, the frontiers that we cross are those that lead into the deepest center of our humanity, where God gazes on us with love. Until we disentangle ourselves from these anxieties and concerns, we do not have the freedom we need to enter into the reality of being human and to find God.

In the image and likeness of God, the pathway to Him is through withdrawing from things not worthy of our dignity and entering into relationship with the One who fashioned our dignity after His own. This is a pathway away from what is visible, comfortable, and familiar and toward what is not visible, comfortable, or familiar. This pathway is torn in faith led by love: not insight or feeling or intuition.

How Saint Teresa of Ávila Crossed the Frontiers of Her Humanity

Teresa of Ávila crossed these frontiers. Even after her conversion and her renewed dedication to prayer, she was still attached to certain friendships which were not spiritually uplifting. Emotional energy and attention that belonged to God, and those whom God had entrusted to her, were dissipated on friendships that did not help her draw close to the Lord or encourage her to do something beautiful for Him with her life. She knew that she needed to renounce and disavow these distracting relationships, but no matter how hard she tried, she found herself pulled back into them.

One of her spiritual friends could not understand how Teresa could possibly enjoy the mystical wisdom that claimed to have been given, but be so immature at the same time. She seemed to experience great tension between what she said she experienced in prayer and the actual fruit of holiness in her life when it came to personal relationships. He was anxious that she might be self-deceived, but the situation was ambiguous.

The Importance of Seeking Counsel

Spiritual discernment consecrates painful ambiguities to God through its surprising discoveries of a deeper love and a greater generosity. It is always possible to come to enough clarity about what is pleasing to God so that we can act on it—if we patiently wait for the Lord to guide us and humbly ask those who He sends our way for sound advice. In this case, how could it be better for Teresa to stop praying? Oftentimes, when it comes to the frontiers of our humanity, consulting others is a necessary part of discernment. This is why Teresa's friend helped her find other spiritually mature and saintly people to counsel her.

One of the spiritual directors that Saint Teresa consulted told her to stop praying. Mental prayer was too dangerous, and she was too sinful. The counsel seemed at first to be persuasive, but Saint Teresa did not feel at peace with it. At the same time, she still did not know what to do. Her friend, however, did not give up on her and helped her find other voices of spiritual authority whose counsel proved more helpful.

There was a new religious community whose founder formed his priests deep in mental prayer as part of their preparation to serve the mission of the Church. Saint Ignatius had experienced his own conversion years before in the mountain monastery of Monserrat. Spiritual exercises or meditations on the life of the Lord were an important part of his original journey in prayer. For several years, he traveled by foot as a pilgrim and eventually spent weeks fasting and praying in a cave outside the town of Manresa, where he developed His spiritual exercises, received powerful visions, but also suffered intense trials in prayer.

He has many powerful insights but one that would benefit our discussion is that when a soul is doing something good, it might not like it at the time, but afterward it feels consoled and even encouraged to greater virtue. Conversely, when a soul is doing something evil, it might at the time really enjoy it, but afterward it feels empty. This is one of the ways to discern whether a course of action that one is following is from God.

When through prayer and discernment we reach a judgment of conscience that we are following the will of God, we should persevere in it for as long as we are convinced that this is true, no matter the circumstances. If it lifts us up and helps us thrive in the long run, even if in the short run it seems tedious, the action may well be something that God is blessing in our lives. If it tears us down in the long run, no matter how good it might feel at the moment, it is a sign that we are involved in something evil and harmful to our integrity. Whenever we become convinced that we are acting falsely or against God's will, it is time to renounce our actions.

What is interesting for this discussion is that we can have a hard time stopping ourselves from doing the harmful thing because evil robs us of our freedom. It saps our liberty so that we have a harder and harder time resisting it. Even though we might recognize that our behavior is wrong and undermining our integrity, without God's help, our freedom to change or even to see the peril of our situation is limited. We are vulnerable to self-deception.

For Teresa, some of the relationships that she was in were clearly evil. They were dragging her down, and she suffered a loss of freedom because of them. Was mental prayer aggravating this, or was God doing something that was not immediately apparent to Saint Teresa or her friend. It was because they discovered the voices of two men of prayer that Saint Teresa finally received the counsel she needed to cross the frontier of her humanity.

A great saint, Francis Borgia, S.J., was one of these voices. A Spanish nobleman, theologian, and widower, Francis gave up his duchy and royal title to become a Jesuit. He was noted not only for his considerable administrative ability but also for his life of contemplation and gifts as a great spiritual director.

Saint Teresa poured out her soul to him and the particular problem she was having with unhealthy relationships. Whereas other spiritual directors were inclined simply to admonish her lack of maturity and direct her to make the difficult renunciation, this contemplative Jesuit took her life of prayer very seriously. The problem was not with the authenticity of her prayer but instead with her lack of confidence in what God was doing in it. Good counsel.

Another spiritual director confirmed what Saint Francis Borgia instructed. With greater familiarity with her situation, he was able to give her even greater insight into how to move forward. Not only was her prayer not the problem, but through prayer, God could act to give her a new freedom. He told her to take the whole matter to prayer by singing the "Veni Creator."

As she raised her heart in this beautiful invocation to the Holy Spirit, her heart was lifted to the Lord in an ecstatic prayer she calls "rapture." Caught up in the love of God, she felt herself freed from the need to be loved by those who were dragging her down.

The point is, in order to pass through our weakness into deeper communion with God, it is not always enough to make a good resolution and then act on it. Sometimes, in difficult renunciations, we must go deeper into prayer and allow the Lord to lift us with His own hands. If we trust the Lord and proceed with confidence in Him, He touches our hearts—pierces them with a fiery dart—and with this fire from above, a greater freedom and fullness of life await us.

The Interior Castle

Entering into silence and solitude is an essential means for growing in contemplative prayer. Conversely mystical wisdom cannot flourish until we journey from living in the periphery of human existence and drawing closer to the presence of God, who dwells in us. After years of contemplative living in the freedom that she discovered through deep prayer, Saint Teresa of Ávila had a vision of the soul that helped her describe and articulate the importance of the wisdom that she had discovered.

She saw a crystal globe surrounded by darkness, and in the center of the globe a beautiful light shone forth. She noticed that the globe was filled with many mansions or dwelling places. There were dwelling places on the outside of the globe, and there were dwelling places on the inside, closer to the center. They were arranged like a castle.

She recognized this vision as an image of the soul. In this spiritual castle, the chambers closer to the center were more luminous and beautiful because of the light. The areas on the peripheries were darker and dangerous because they were farther from the light. Out of this image Teresa developed her whole spiritual doctrine contained in her classic *Interior Castle*. It is a journey from the peripheries of our existence into the center, where the light of God shines in our hearts.

In Teresa's vision, the soul is filled with light in the inside and shines in a darkness that surrounds it. The different chambers of this castle disclose a grave truth about human existence. Although there are many things that happen in life that we have no control over, we can always decide whether or not we will rise to the greatness of our vocation. God has summoned us into existence as human beings, and He leaves it up to us whether we will respond to our highest calling. Each of us has a solemn choice to make: whether to live centered in our humanity or in the peripheries of it.

God's presence calls us out of the peripheries and into a deeper experience of our own identity and mission as creatures in His image and likeness. He created us to be a dwelling place for His presence. The human vocation, the pathway to a more fully lived life, is to draw close to God in the midst of darkness.

Each moment and every situation leaves us with a choice: Will we live our lives closer to the darkness beyond the Lord's warmth and radiance? Or, will we journey to dwell near the light so that we can realize our vocation to be a place for God to shine?

There is an important corollary regarding the dignity of our human vocation that Saint Teresa's vision also suggests. Drawing close to God is not a matter of withdrawing from our humanity. Instead, it is a matter of entering into the human experience more fully. Seeking the Lord's presence in our hearts opens up the possibility of living to the full the life He gives to us.

Without the light of God, our earthly life can be a cold, loveless void of meaninglessness. This light burns in the center of our humanity, but when we do not consider who we are and who dwells in us, we are distracted by many meaningless things. When we avoid our humanity, we lose the only reference point that we have to find God's presence.

Weighed down by a burden of guilt, we are not at ease with ourselves or the world, and we are not sure what to do about it. We yearn with unfulfilled desires to be connected with something that does not pass away while our existence rushes toward alienation, infertility, and all kinds of bodily weakness.

In this absence of truth and love, it is difficult to trust God, and we are left grasping for control and security in life. It is true, even of very pious and devout people, that we can be so good about controlling people and situations that we do not know how out of control we really are. Driven by all kinds of brokenness, some of which we have inherited and some of which we have brought on ourselves, we constantly forget the fire of God's presence within us.

Teresa's vision helps us consider that we will not be truly at rest with ourselves until we cross this threshold of a deeper confidence in God. This starts with a humble recognition of the disparity between how we now live and how the Lord calls us to live: in the deepest center of our humanity, where he waits for us. If we ask God, He can help us see how carried away we are by our self-perception or the perception that others have of us. He can help us question why we exhaust ourselves on the edges of life and why we subject ourselves to all kinds of confusion. It frightened Teresa of Ávila to discover that when our desires for control and security are not given to the Lord, we can easily become slaves to the whims of our ego or the egos of others.

As we struggle with this disparity in our lives, God can begin to draw us closer to His presence. This is what the Church means by mystical wisdom, by growing in our awareness of the presence of God. Contemplative prayer attempts not to surmount our humanity but to face the obstacles to being fully human and fully alive. It is freedom from what is comfortable and convenient so that we can draw closer to the light and warmth of God.

The pathway through this wilderness is cut by a deeper work of prayer. This more interior form of prayer pulls us out of ourselves and makes us vulnerable to God. This is a secret contemplation. Saint John of the Cross calls it a dark contemplation and a ray of darkness.

Beyond our conscious awareness, the Holy Spirit operates in the incomprehensible depths of our personal existence. He heals and restores, expands and makes beautiful, depths that we do not know about in our hearts. Such a grace is more powerful than the dynamism of self, and we find ourselves preoccupied with something much more wonderful: Someone beyond our power to understand.

We withdraw into prayer and take up spiritual battle for this kind of freedom. Unaware of His action, we withdraw to surrender to the silent melodies of His love. By withdrawing, we learn a simple movement of the will, an act of trust that clings to Him in the spiritual darkness to which He has allured us. The self no longer occupies us because we are rendered forgetful of everything but God. Here, we find the freedom to be vulnerable to His love.

This is the night Saint John of the Cross celebrates. Everything that is not for the glory of God, including our tendency to fuss over ourselves, must be renounced so that we can enter into this night. Our own efforts, however, only prepare the way for a new work that God begins. In the sheer grace of the night God blesses us with, an enchanting silence catches us off guard, and we are drawn into a loving mystery.

Self-denial and renunciation of even very good things allow us to withdraw our hearts into the space Christ needs to disclose His love in the night. Renouncing all manner of natural relationships is never done because there is something wrong with those we naturally love. It is rather out of devotion to Christ and the desire to imitate Him more perfectly that some renounce family life to embrace a supernatural society, such as monastic life. To do this, they also embrace a certain anonymity in which the uniqueness of who they are is hidden to everyone except the Lord. They do this because they have found a secret joy that far outweighs the sorrow and hardship such sacrifices occasion.

What is most curious to me is that those who embrace this anonymity have powerfully deep personalities. It is as if renouncing being known by others has made them free to become more fully themselves. What seems to happen is that those who give up trying to find their identity in what others think of them are free to discover who they really are in relation to God. One really knows himself only in relation to the Lord, and only as one knows the truth about himself does prayer become more and more real and vital. Those who choose this as their life's priority are living signs for all those who want to learn to pray.

Solitude and silence free the heart to attend to God. This liberation requires time. The journey of prayer is a pilgrimage out of not only exterior noise but also interior cacophony. Anything that is out of harmony distracts from the still, small voice of God, whether in the external world around us or in the interior world of our feelings and thoughts. Discouragement, self-pity, righteous indignation, resentment, anxiety over worldly occupa-tions—this is all internal noise. Such noise can drown out the gentle breeze in which the Lord speaks. We must not allow our hearts to be caught up in the currents of such storms.

13

THE NEED FOR MERCIFUL LOVE

In the weeks before World Youth Day, the media in Denver dubbed the summer of 1993 "the summer of violence." There were gang shootings that took the lives of many young people, not far from the boundaries of our parish. No one was sure what to do about the situation or even how to pray about it, but our pastor, Fr. Marcian O'Meara, and several parishioners felt we must do something.

We decided to invite all the youth of the city to an evening of prayer. It was hoped that if young people prayed for peace, the Lord would bring peace back to the community. We discovered together that the gift of peace is not something the Lord grants to the half-hearted. Peace is a gift from above, and it is given only to those who ask with earnest faith.

A Franciscan priest, Fr. Stan Fortuna, C.F.R., came from New York to lead us in a holy hour. He and the other Franciscan Friars of the Renewal have worked for peace in difficult neighborhoods throughout New York for years. Surely, he would be able to show our community how to pray.

Disappointingly, only a few young people and their families came for the event. Fr. Stan was unperturbed by this turnout. He began the evening by making the Sign of the Cross and kneeling in the sanctuary before the altar and the cross.

He cried out from his heart. I do not remember the exact words he used. But what he did say helped all of us realize the preciousness of the gift we were asking for and how unworthy we were to ask for it. He said something like, "Lord, have mercy on me and on everyone gathered here in prayer. How often we have failed to pray for peace when other communities were touched by violence. Only now when violence threatens our own neighborhood do we come to ask Your help. Who are we to dare to come before You and ask for Your peace?"

He went on to ask the Lord to forgive us for our indifference. Those of us at this vigil for peace suddenly saw the reality of our situation. When violence and suffering affected others, we were indifferent. Now, only when it affected us, did we come and ask the Lord for His peace.

In other words, one of the reasons we did not have the peace of God in our community was that instead of going to God with humility, we had for some time dared to approach Him with indifference. This indifference impeded the Lord from pouring out His peace on us. This prayer service was an actual grace for radical conversion away from indifference. It was a call to be connected with the Lord and with one another in a deeper way.

Fr. Stan helped us see our own coldness of heart and need for conversion. He helped us begin to pray from the place where we really were. Those few who participated in this event remembered this prayer when, during and after World Youth Day, there was a dramatic decrease in crime and violence across the city.

The violence we suffer or inflict on others can be dealt with only when we submit it to the one who violently suffered for our offenses. Our indifference to the plight of others comes into relief before this mystery, and here there are important questions to ask ourselves. This inner questioning is part of real prayer, a true ongoing encounter with Christ.

The Growing Face of Violence Today

These many years later, I would like to think that the grace we received at the prayer vigil at Good Shepherd Parish was also a grace spreading throughout our community. It is not that simple. My memory goes to Columbine High School (already several years ago now).

In frenzied brutality and aggression, a couple of demented teenage boys indulged in a frenzy of senseless hatred. Blinded by both cruelty and cowardice, they unleashed their fury on their helpless peers. Innocent young people were brutally murdered. Some were actually martyred because of their Christian faith.

In the days and weeks that followed, I went to the parishes in the area, wanting to help. Students and parents were in shock, others in tears. Priests, deacons, and laity were pouring themselves out and making themselves available.

At first, I did not know what to do, and I felt powerless. Violence had again touched our community—and again we were all in prayer, questioning where we really stood before Lord. It was time to be present to the heroic young people who were grieving. They needed someone to listen to them, to console them, and, most of all, to pray with them. They needed a word of hope in the midst of the bitter ambiguity into which their lives had suddenly plunged.

What is this bitterness the unconscionable acts of violent aggression perpetrated by angry young men have caused? What is the bitterness that moves these young people with such malice? There may be a connection, and this connection may be something more than the sum total of the psychological and sociological circumstances surrounding each case.

Suburban school and theater shootings are essentially the same spectacular and cowardly violence plaguing much of the Middle East and Africa in the form of Islamic uprisings. What are identified as coordinated terrorist attacks Europe's great cities are simply large-scale versions of violent gang activity in America's dismal urban sprawl. In a certain sense, it is all brutally irrational whether or not specific sociological and psychological pathologies are involved.

This destructive rage is indulged in for the sake of spectacle— a lust for celebrity as well as the euphoric sense of control. With calculated cowardice it targets the unsuspecting and helpless. The nihilistic end justifies the brutal means—consciously or unconsciously. This evil, however, is much deeper than this.

Both affluent suburbia and impoverished urban ghettos seem to incubate this hatred. Disconnected, alienated, and overly indulged, a tormented soul that stokes contempt is unable to choose anything else freely. Freedom comes only in the form of a love that is willing to enter into and patiently suffer this deep ache. If we wait, however, until this kind of needy beggar comes knocking at our door, we have missed the great calling of our lives.

Contemplative Prayer as an Answer to Hatred

The Lord told Catherine de Hueck Doherty that she was to go boldly into the hearts of others. This is the way forward today—the true answer to the violence of our time. We cannot do this alone. He who is risen from the dead goes before us in this great project. Our job is to follow prayerfully in His footsteps.

I write this now with a certain sense of urgency. Current policies at work in our government want to limit religion to the private sphere. Catholic hospitals, schools, and other works of charity that are now part of the public square are being squeezed out. The Little Sisters of the Poor, who have given up marriage and everything else to care for the elderly, are now engaged in a legal fight with the United States government that may end up defining this issue for a generation.

The irony is, now more than ever, that our society needs communities like the Little Sisters. America and the world need us to bring the gospel of Christ to our cities and our suburbs, to public places, including our schools, to make our faith a living part of our community. Without our Catholic faith and especially our Christian prayer, our culture aches with a misery it cannot manage.

In the face of senseless violence, we must renew our courage to pray and deepen our confidence in the mercy that comes from God. We need the wisdom that Christian prayer unleashes in our lives and in the world. This kind of prayer discerns how our misery is drawing down God's mercy, and it recognizes that His mercy has the form of the Cross.

This kind of prayer helps us find the most appropriate way to serve God in the midst of the painful ambiguities of life. In contemplation we find the courage and strength to make the sacrifices love requires and to stand firm in the mercy of God. In this wisdom we become confident that the Cross stands in the center of the world and reigns over everything, over every situation.

The Victory of Good over Evil

Here, contemplative prayer brings us into apocalyptic reality. Each moment of prayer is intimately realized eschatology. In fact, deep prayer fully anticipates the final judgment and leads us into the mystery of mercy. This is why those who pray discover heroic levels of courage and deep internal resolve. No matter what unravels around them, they stand on the Word, the Word made flesh. Just as the Lord preached: "Sun and moon may pass away" but the Word of the Lord, His promise fulfilled in Christ Jesus, "will never fail."[55]

Mystical wisdom born in contemplative prayer beholds the Lord Jesus Christ. It ponders the example He gave us. It sees in impossible situations how to sanctify the dirt and grit of life by prayer. Because He is eternally God, He was able to sow a new experience of divine power in the depths of this mud. In mental prayer, what He sowed can sprout anew in us.

This kind of wisdom is united to His cry to the Father. It answers the aggression that is at work in our hearts. His sacrifice of thanksgiving gives us the freedom to choose another way. The praise of glory that He offers overcomes evil with good, and by contemplative prayer, this offering is a mystery in which we also implicate ourselves.

Mystical wisdom is not a future possibility but a reality present in the Church for us today. Since Christ continues to unleash the unvanquished power of Divine Love even today, in this moment, at the right hand of the Father, our own efforts to join our hearts to His are never without value. For this reason, the dynamism of Christ's prayer is both a historical reality and ever-unfolding mystical power until the end of time. In union with His prayer, evil finds its limit and mercy is extended in new and unexpected ways.

---

[55] For a beautiful reflection on this point, see Pope Benedict XVI, *Jesus of Nazareth, Part Two: Holy Week: from the Entrance into Jerusalem to the Resurrection*, trans. Philip J. Whitmore (San Francisco: Ignatius Press, 2011), 49–52.

Only as we spend time in prayer, allowing Him to disclose His great love for us, is He finally free to share with us this great purpose, this spiritual mission. What the great mission might be for any particular soul is such a beautiful and profound mystery that no book can possibly help one to understand it. It is a reality between the soul and God, something He speaks deep in the substance of the soul's being.

The Mission of Mental Prayer

In the name of the Father, Christ sends His disciples into the world in the power of the Holy Spirit to make known the mercies of God. The humble movement of God's heart reaching out to ours, extending even into the deepest recesses of our misery, ought to evoke our love and gratitude. Those who come to realize what Christ suffered for their sakes yearn to give a return. They are so overcome by how much they are loved by Christ that they are willing to do anything for Him. They want to imitate Him in everything. We find this sentiment in the prayers and reflections of Blessed Charles de Foucauld, who wanted to imitate in his own heart all the movements of the Heart of Jesus:

> My Father, I abandon myself into Your hands. Make of me whatever You please. Whatever You do with me, I thank You: I am ready for all and I accept all; only let Your Will be done in me, my God. Provided that Your will be done in all Your creatures, all Your children, all those whom Your Heart loves, I desire nothing else, my God. Into Your hands I commend my spirit, and I give it to You, my God, with all the love of my heart. I love You, and I give myself to You for the sake of this love in me. Into Your

s, I entrust myself without measure, with an infinite confidence, because You are my Father.[56]

Blessed Charles wrote this prayer while meditating on Luke 23:46 — the prayer of Jesus on the Cross. It is the most powerful of all prayers ever offered. It was the prayer that Blessed Charles wanted as the heartbeat of his own life. This kind of union with Christ's prayer is filled with wisdom in the face of apparent defeat, a wisdom that he in fact witnessed to in his own ministry.

As a priest and hermit, he worked for the conversion of the Taureg People in North Africa. They were Muslim, but not very devout, and he had hoped to win their hearts to Christ by showing them the mercy of God through his own kindness to them. Blessed Charles befriended them and gently entered into their lives. No one ever converted as a result of his efforts, but many were impressed with the hermit. Then there was an uprising, and the old hermit was betrayed by a friend, attacked by soldiers, and shot in the back by a frightened teenager. It seemed as though his whole life had been a failure.

Yet his abandonment to the Father and his life of prayer would influence many of the new religious movements throughout the twentieth century. Why was he so fruitful in the face of so much failure? To make this movement in the heart of Christ the movement of one's own heart is to allow oneself to be as rejected and hated as was the Lord Himself. The more rejected and the more Christlike we become, the more fruitful our prayer becomes — even in ways we do not expect it to. Mental prayer in the Christian tradition leads to this solidarity with the Lord.

---

[56] *La Prière d'abandon*, January 23, 1897.

It is the mystery of the Cross that unlocks the power of mercy in the world.

Primal hostility toward God in our culture and in the lives of individuals is directed at the person who is holy. This is the reason Blessed Charles was betrayed to his murderers. It is why great saints such as Maximilian Kolbe and Teresa Benedicta of the Cross were killed in Auschwitz. It seems this is really the reason Saint John Paul II was shot. It is also the reason he went into prison, embraced the man who shot him, and prayed with him. What does this mean for those who want to live with fire from above? Saint John of the Cross says, "Where there is no love, put love, and you will draw out love."[57]

---

[57] See Letter 26, in *Complete Works*, 760.

14

FORGIVENESS AND CONTEMPLATION

One obstacle to beginning to pray and living within is the struggle to forgive. Whenever someone hurts us in a serious way, there is a spiritual wound that remains. As we begin to pray, we commonly find ourselves going back over these wounds again and again. What is most frustrating is that many times we thought we had already forgiven the person who hurt us. But when the memory comes back, we can sometimes feel the anger and the pain all over again.

What do we do with the wounds so that they no longer impede our ability to pray? The *Catechism of the Catholic Church* explains, "It is not in our power not to feel or to forget an offense; but the heart that offers itself to the Holy Spirit turns injury into compassion and purifies the memory in transforming hurt into intercession" (CCC 2843).

To pray for those who have hurt us is difficult. In scriptural terms, those who hurt us are our enemies, and this is true even when they are friends and close family members. Christ commands us to love our enemies and to do good to those who persecute us. Betrayal, abandonment, indifference, scandal, abuse, scorn, sarcasm, ridicule, detraction, and insult—these are all bitter things to forgive. The Lord grieves with us and for us when we suffer these things. He has permitted us to suffer them for a profound reason.

The Lord explained to His disciples that those who hunger and thirst for the sake of justice, those who are merciful, and especially those who are persecuted for righteousness and for the Lord are blessed. Their mysterious beatitude makes sense only when we see through the eyes of faith the injustice and persecution they have endured. Somehow, trusting in God in the midst of such things makes them in the likeness of Christ. Trusting in God means to pray for those who harm us, to seek to return good for evil. When this act of trust is made, the power of God is released in humanity. For two thousand years, this is what every martyr for our faith has revealed to the Church.

Why God Permits the
Persecution of Those He Loves

In his mysterious wisdom and profound love, when the Father allows someone to hurt or oppose us in some way, He is entrusting that person to our prayers. When our enemy causes us to suffer unjustly, our faith tells us that this was allowed to happen so that we might participate in the mystery of the Cross. Somehow, like those who offered their lives for our faith, the mystery of redemption is being renewed through our own sufferings.

We have a special authority over the soul of someone who causes us great sorrow. Their actions have bound them to us in the mercy of God. Mercy is love that suffers the evil of another to affirm his dignity so that he does not have to suffer alone.[58]

---

[58] See Saint Thomas Aquinas, *Summa Theologica* II-II, Q. 30, art. 1.

Whenever someone hurts us physically or even emotionally, he has demeaned himself even more. He is even more in need of mercy.

From this perspective, the injury our enemies have caused us can be a gateway for us to embrace the even greater sufferings with which their hearts are burdened. Because of this relationship, our prayers on their behalf have a particular power. The Father hears these prayers because prayer for our enemies enters deep into the mystery of the Cross. But how do we begin to pray for our enemies when the very thought of them and what they have done stirs our hearts with bitterness and resentment?

Here we must ask what it means to repent for our lack of mercy. The first step is the hardest. Whether they are living or dead, we need to forgive those who have hurt us. This is the hardest because forgiveness involves more than intellectually assenting to the fact that we ought to forgive.

We know that we get some pleasure out of our grievances. The irrational pleasure we can sometimes take in these distracts us from what God Himself desires us to do. What happens when all that pleasure is gone, when all we have left is the Cross? Saint John of the Cross sees our poverty in the midst of great affliction as the greatest union with Christ crucified possible in this life: "When they are reduced to nothing, the highest degree of humility, the spiritual union between their souls and God will be an accomplished fact. This union is most noble and sublime state attainable in this life." In the face of our grievances we must realize this solidarity with Christ and cleave to His example with all our strength.[59]

---

[59] Saint John of the Cross, *Ascent of Mount Carmel* 2:7:11, in *Complete Works*, 172.

Living by the Cross means choosing, over and over, whenever angry and resentful memories come up, not to hold a debt against someone who has hurt us. It means renouncing secret vows of revenge to which we have bound ourselves. It means avoiding indulging in self-pity or thinking ill of those who have sinned against us. It means begging God to show us the truth about our enemy's plight.

The Work of the Holy Spirit

Here, human effort alone cannot provide the healing such ongoing choices demand. Only the Lord's mercy can dissolve our hardness of heart toward those who have harmed us. We have to surrender our grievances to the Holy Spirit, who turns "injury into compassion" and transforms "hurt into intercession" (CCC 2849).

As with every Christian who has tried to follow Him, the Cross terrified Jesus. He sweat blood in the face of it. We believe that it was out of the most profound love for us and for His Father that He embraced this suffering. Because of this love, He would not have it any other way. Overcoming His own fear, He accepted death for our sake and, in accepting it, sanctified it so that it might become the pathway to new life.

Precisely because Jesus has made death a pathway of life, Christians are also called to take up their crosses and follow Him. They must offer up their resentment to God and allow their bitterness to die. Offering the gift of our grievances to God is especially pleasing to Him. It is part of our misery, and our misery is the only thing we really have to offer God that He wants.

This effort is spiritual, the work of the Holy Spirit. In order to forgive, we must pray, and sometimes we must devote many hours, days, and even years to prayer for this purpose. It is a difficult part of our conversatio morum. Yet we cannot dwell very deep in our hearts, we cannot live with ourselves, if we do not find mercy for those who have offended us. Living with ourselves, living within ourselves, is impossible without mercy.

There are moments in such prayer when we suddenly realize we must not only forgive but must also ask for forgiveness. A transformation takes place when our attention shifts from the evil done to us to the plight of the person who inflicted it. Every time we submit resentment to the Lord, every time we renounce a vengeful thought, every time we offer the Lord the deep pain in our heart, even if we do not feel or understand it, we have made room for the gentle action of the Holy Spirit.

The Holy Spirit does not take the wounds away. They remain like the wounds in the hands and side of Christ. The wounds of Christ are a pathway into the heart of every man and woman. This is because the hostility of each one of us toward Him caused those wounds. Similarly when someone wounds us, the wound can become a pathway into that person's heart. Wounds bind us to those who have hurt us, especially those who have become our enemies, because whenever someone hurts us, he has allowed us to share in his misery, to know the lack of love he suffers. With the Holy Spirit, this knowledge is a powerful gift.

Once the Holy Spirit shows us this truth, we have a choice. We can choose to suffer this misery with the one who hurt us in prayer so that God might restore that person's dignity. When we choose this, our wounds, like the wounds of Christ, no longer dehumanize as long as we do not backslide. Instead, the Holy Spirit transforms such wounds into founts of grace. Those who have experienced this will tell you that with the grace of Christ there is no room for bitterness. There is only great compassion and sober prayerfulness.

Saint Thomas Aquinas on
Mercy and the Gift of Counsel

As we go further into the discussion of Saint Thomas Aquinas on mercy, he explains that the Holy Spirit's gift of counsel is a special prompting, or impetus, in the heart that brings every act of mercy to perfection.[60] The gift of counsel, explains Saint Thomas, allows us to know and to understand the misery in the hearts of others. Once we know and understand their misery, we can bind ourselves to them in prayer so that those who have hurt us might feel the mercy of God in their misery, that they might find a reason to hope, a pathway out of the hell in which they are imprisoned.

It is by this same gift that Christ knew our hostility to God and allowed Himself to be wounded unto death by it. He wanted to bear this dehumanizing force in our nature so that it might die with Him. This way, when He rose again, He could free from futility all that is good, noble, and true about each of us.

Likewise with us, this same gift allows us to extend Christ's saving work into the hearts of others. In particular, the gift of counsel allows us to understand the dehumanizing hostility others have unleashed on us and by understanding it in faith, to offer it to God in love. When we do this, our mercy, perfected by the Holy Spirit, makes space in the hearts of those who have hurt us, space into which God's love can flow. It is the saving mercy of God, His love suffering our misery, which is the only hope for humanity.

---

[60] See Saint Thomas Aquinas, *Summa Theologica* II-II, Q. 30, art. 1; Q. 52, art. 4.

15

MENTAL PRAYER AND SPIRITUAL EXERCISES

Contemplative prayer captures the heart in love and leaves it in a kind of speechless wonder that it does not understand. Mental or contemplative prayer for Teresa of Ávila involves attentiveness to the presence of God. In her efforts to be attentive to Him, she meditated on Christ within her or read a spiritual book to place herself in the presence of God. These spiritual exercises dispose the heart for deeper kinds of contemplation.

While doing this, Teresa would oftentimes experience the Lord suddenly making Himself felt in such a way that she could no longer doubt that He was in her or that she was totally immersed in Him. She sometimes even felt suspended outside herself in love unable to remember or think about anything but Him. She explained that the only understanding of this she enjoyed was that she knew she understood nothing about it. His presence was too immense, too beautiful, and too intimate to understand. She identifies this experience as "mystical theology."[61]

She recommends two kinds of spiritual exercises for disposing ourselves to the Lord's presence. We can think about Jesus and various scenes of His life, or we can carefully examine our

---

[61] Saint Teresa of Ávila, *The Book of Her Life*, 104.

lives and search for His presence in our memories. Both of these efforts to meditate open up moments of deep intimacy with the Lord. This spiritual exercise of our imagination, understanding, and affectivity renders us mindful of Him.

During meditation, in very gentle and profound ways, sometimes noticed and sometimes not, He touches us when we try to exercise sincere and mindful devotion. As we call to mind the Passion of Christ, the thought of Him who was pierced for our offenses can also pierce us. As we call to mind His mercy in our lives, we find countless instances of His kindness for which the only proper response is sober gratitude and adoration.

Contemplative Prayer and Distractions

Contemplative prayer involves a determined effort to attend to the Lord and to allow the heart to rest in the things of God. Saint Teresa's conversion involved ongoing dedication to this kind of prayer. She strove to make her days begin with holy thoughts and desires worthy of the Lord. She would baptize her imagination and her intellect by reading teachings on prayer and the wisdom of the saints.

Her effort was not to work herself up into an emotional state. Compunction is evoked, not produced. This holy sorrow is a gift, the response of the heart to something the Lord has to say. Saint Teresa's effort to meditate was instead a matter of learning to listen.

For Saint Teresa, mental prayer is nothing other than a holy conversation with God. Like any worthwhile conversation, in order to have something worthwhile to say, we must listen. In the case of mental prayer, listening involves a special attentiveness to the mystery of God's presence with all the powers of our being.

Mental prayer is the effort to render one's whole existence vulnerable to truths so unfathomable that they can only be received and accepted, but never fully grasped. This kind of prayer does not aim at achieving a spiritual or psychic state. It is not primarily ordered toward attaining enlightened consciousness. It is a simple and humble movement of trust, a seeking of the truth in love. The proper use of spiritual exercises in this kind of prayer consists, therefore, in the humble effort to welcome the truth.

We can be pierced to the heart only when we learn to listen with this kind of obedience. Such attentiveness is a radical availability to the will of God over and above the projections of our own ego and personal projects. Beyond any scheme for self-improvement, this obedient readiness to respond to God requires a prayerful receptivity. This total availability of a listening heart "sees" or "contemplates" God because nothing in such a heart obscures His self-disclosure.

How do we discipline ourselves to listen to God rightly? We return to Saint Teresa's image of prayerful meditation as drawing water from a well. We need to embrace spiritual exercises that turn our attention to the Lord anew. As we noted at the beginning of this discussion, this means pondering the mysteries of Christ's life or mystery of Christ revealed in our own life story.

When our minds are scattered on unholy and frivolous things before prayer, a simple firm decision to attend to the presence of God is a good first step. Sometimes we need to be determined not to allow our minds to wander into problem solving or into entertaining fantasies. Instead, out of love for the Lord, we resolve that this time that we have set aside for God belongs to Him alone.

picture or the Bible or a good book on prayer can help us renounce these distractions. Gazing on an icon or a crucifix helps dispose our senses and imagination to this conversation with God. Thoughtfully repeating a Scripture verse or recounting moments in the life of the Lord opens our minds to this contemplative work. Then, closing our eyes, we can also think about holy things until we are filled with wonder. Perseverance in this effort, even when peppered with distraction, is already the beginning of mental prayer.

In addition to thinking about the life of the Lord, we can also reflect on all the wonderful ways God is present in our lives. Saint Augustine's *Confessions*, a work very dear to Teresa of Ávila, is filled with this kind of prayer. He looks back and sees all that the Lord has done in the face of his own sin. He confesses the folly of his pride to help us see the righteousness of God. He confesses his sexual struggles and weakness so that we might understand the greatness of purity and God's strength in us. His journey into prayer became a journey into truth, goodness, beauty, and life—and he witnesses in all of this that the Lord spoke to him personally, not with human speech, but with words that pierced the very marrow of his being.

In many ways, Saint Teresa of Ávila's autobiographical work, *La Vida*, is the same kind of work that the *Confessions* represents. Like Augustine, we find her recounting events from her past life and marveling at the ways God was so close to her even when she was very far from God. This goes beyond a mere autobiography. It is a personal witness to what happens when a soul finally listens to the Lord.

Personal reflection on her own life was a moment of prayer for her. This gave her a new occasion to submit all her memories and struggles to the Lord all over again and to discover in deeper ways the beautiful work that He was accomplishing in her. Like these saints, we have so much to be thankful for, and we are so little aware of all that God has done.

This kind of mental prayer is almost always possible when we are honest with ourselves. This is true even when our hearts do not seem to feel what they should when we think about holy things. Whether we contemplate Christ dying for us on the Cross or whether we turn our attention to the Lord's mysterious presence in our neighbor, this raising of our mind to God and the things of God is already the threshold of prayer.

Cultivating a Love for Silence

Saint Teresa learned that, although in the beginning drawing up this spiritual water took a lot of effort and determination, at a certain stage it became easier and easier for her to rest in the loving awareness of God's presence. She called this ability to rest in God's presence the prayer of quiet.

Such prayer is the holy recollection of the powers of our soul in Christ, a silent stillness before the mystery of His presence, and an adoring openness to His generous love. It is like standing at the threshold of heaven. In her reflection on the Lord's Prayer, Saint Teresa turns our attention to the immanent presence of our heavenly Father — a reality she insists that we must not only believe but also understand by lived experience:

> Withdraw into solitude and look for Him within. Do not neglect so good a Guest. With great humility, instead, speak to Him as to a father. Tell Him about your trials, ask Him for help, and realize that you are not worthy.[62]

---

[62] See Saint Teresa of Ávila, *The Way of Perfection* 28:1.

Along the same lines Saint John of the Cross encourages:

> Rejoice and enjoy your interior recollection with Him, for He is so close to you. Desire Him within, adore Him there.[63]

---

[63] Saint John of the Cross, *Spiritual Canticle* 1:8.

16

REASON LIFTED
UP IN PRAYER

In a world strangled by all kinds of irrationality, prayer lifts up the power of reason above its natural limits for the glory of God. Earlier in this work, we reflected on the role of faith in prayer. This chapter builds on those insights to explore the mindfulness of Christian prayer.

In Christian prayer, a meaningful conversation with God is possible because the Creator of human rationality has made a special place for right thinking in His eternal plan. The role of intelligence in the plan of God is of vital importance in the life of prayer.

Mindful prayer is against mindlessness. Speaking to God does not require that we check our intelligence at the door and indulge in meaningless twaddle clothed in pious language. Just the opposite. Christians are not to be empty minded. We are not simply to go along with the way everyone else thinks and mindlessly agree with the latest social convention.

The mindfulness of Christian prayer trains us to live by what we do not fully see. When others are paralyzed in despair, Christians must be ready with a word of hope. Through the effort to pray, the Christian mind learns to behold the world with resurrected eyes.

True prayer requires the highest cognitive functions, even in the most simple of heart. This is not a matter of superior analytical or synthetic reasoning skills. It is instead about beholding the truth and allowing this vision to purify and intensify our humanity. The use of reason in prayer is about putting on the mind of Christ and knowing the mind of God. In fact, the simpler and purer the soul, the more heavenly its intellectual acts become.

The role of reason in prayer according to Saint Thomas Aquinas supports this position. One of the most powerful intellects in the history of the Church, he did not see the gift of reason at odds with the humility of prayer. Instead, the Angelic Doctor proposes that the etymology of prayer suggests a rich connection between prayer and reason. Prayer, or *oratio*, could be called a mouthful of reason, *oris ratio* (reason of the mouth): *oratio dicitur quasi oris ratio*.[64]

For Saint Thomas Aquinas prayer and reason are not in opposition but are ordered to each other. Grace-filled reason provides for the essential character of Christian prayer. This is because Christian prayer in its most basic form is a petition, a cry of the heart. Reason fills this cry with meaning before God when reason suffers the truth about our situation before Him.

Reason is the power to attend to, to judge, and to share the secrets of our hearts and to allow what others disclose to us to shape and refine our judgments. This is the power to see and deepen relations—relations between the circumstances of the moment, our needs, the needs of others, and divine providence. When these relations are expressed and shared with God, the truth is disclosed in a way that allows God to act.

[64] "Prayer is like reason from the mouth." Saint Thomas Aquinas, *Summa Theologica* II-II, Q. 83, art. 1.

God has chosen to act in the spiritual "space" that a humble petition creates in the universe. In fact, there are certain things that He will do only when we avail our lives to Him in humble petition. Wonderful blessings are in store, but in accord with the wisdom and goodness of His plan, He humbly waits and does not coerce. In this way, He has placed great confidence in humanity, relying on our prayer to accomplish His hidden purpose.

Prayer is a conversation. A good conversation requires discernment, awareness of what is appropriate and what is not, a mutual attentiveness. Reason in prayer attends to who we are, what we are asking, and from Whom we are asking. If reason is limited to its earthly powers, such attentiveness and connection to God is impossible. But when the mind is raised by God above itself into heavenly perspectives, grace-filled reason avails itself to transformative moments of personal encounter.

Catechesis and doctrinal formation help raise reason into this kind of conversation. Through the teaching of the Church, reason is given the help it needs to see the heart's desires and to express these to the Lord in a meaningful and appropriate way. Prayer is not meaningful if it does not reach into the desires of our hearts. Our catechesis helps us affirm the truth about the great mystery of God and discern the desires, guilt, and experience of death with which our prayers are concerned.

Prayer Is Not an Impulse to Emptiness

Not everyone agrees with this doctrinal vision of prayer. Some argue that since God already knows our deepest needs, sharing these with Him is redundant. Instead of humble petition, some teachers suggest emptying the mind of everything. As rationality is abandoned, they propose that the mind can evolve beyond limiting structures.

For them, catechesis and the teaching of the Church are a helpful stepping-stone, but the impulse of the mind toward nothingness will take a soul into a more enlightened consciousness. They believe that divine revelation is not important in itself but only as a helpful form to get started. They recommend simply getting in touch with the impulse of will toward the Absolute. In this deliberate silencing of all thoughts and desires, they promise that reason and desire can be surmounted, and they advocate a plunge into mystery that is beyond a personal experience of the divine.

Some mystics use language that sounds like what these teachers propose, but they do not adhere to this vision of prayer. No saintly authority proposes that the Trinity is only the appearance of God for Christians. Their vision of prayer is not the heart intending emptiness or an impulse to a nonpersonal absolute.

Christian mysticism is intrinsically relational. We are not isolated monads whose mere intention is to have power to shape the world or even our lives. The alienation of sin and death does not define our existence. Our prayer is not closed in on its own intentions and impulses, because Christ crucified has gained access to our hearts and suffered their truth. He opens up access to God for our whole embodied spirit—from the heights of our rationality and the depths of our affectivity, from the furthest bodily extremity to the very substance of the soul.

Before the Cross, mere intention and impulse are not enough. A more complete and more human total response is required. The Cross is where the love of the Father and the prayers of humanity collide—and Christian prayer is all about this love as a lived reality. It is a reality lived in relationship, in connection with God and those the Lord gives us. In the image and likeness of the Trinity, we are beings "in relation" to one another and to

God — and the power of reason is ordered to these personal relations and the divine harmony God alone can establish in them.

Although it is true that holy desires move us to pray,[65] prayer
itself extends beyond desire and engages all the powers of our
soul, purifying them and expanding them beyond all expectation. In this way, prayer is the highest and noblest of all human
activities, the activity that involves the free engagement of the
highest functions of our intelligence to their fullest potential
and this on the most important, most vital matters of existence.

The Cosmic Place of Prayer and Reason

In God's eyes, one human thought, filled with faith, is worth
more than the whole tangible world.[66] Because of the unique
place of humanity in the center of the visible cosmos, the prayer
of faith establishes true order — from the most interior realities
of the heart to the concrete physical circumstances of the world
in which we dwell. This is because prayer is in a special way
an act of grace-permeated reason. In this healed and expanded
rational power, humble human thought is raised into the mind
of God by the Word of the Father and set on fire by the gift of
the Holy Spirit.

Through reason raised in prayer, God brings both the soul and
the world into harmony with His divine plan. In prayer that is
worthy of God, human reason participates with Divine Reason,
the Word of the Father. A humble word can be a powerful thing
if said in the right way, at the right time, to the right person and
for the right reason. This is because a word, even in frail human
speech, mediates truth; it has the power to convey the truth

---

[65] See Saint Augustine, Letter 130, to Proba.
[66] See Saint John of the Cross, *Sayings of Light and Love*, no. 35.

with love. In prayer, this mediation accesses the mystery of God Himself, and He uses it to bring to completion His great purpose.

Human Reason and the Reason of God

Grace-filled reason is moved by the Holy Spirit to order our thinking to the Word made flesh so that we might ask in His Name. Jesus Christ mediates the love of the Father. He is the harmony of God echoing in our humanity.

This primordial creative Word of the Father is eternal and undying. He is the Father's final Word about human existence. This word fills us with the words of prayer, even when human speech fails to articulate what He discloses in our spirit. Reason raised in prayer dances with Eternal Truth, in whom alone is found light, life, and love. Prayer asks for things from God by giving Him the spiritual space to answer in a manner that reveals His glory and goodness.

The Gospel of John reveals Jesus as the Logos of the Father. We translate this as "Word." In Greek, however, *Logos* is more than what we mean by "word." Logos is the reason, the rationality, the relation, the harmony, the mediation of what is known with what truly is. In the Word of the Father, we have the ultimate truth that resonates throughout creation, has suffered the consequences of sin, and has conquered death.

When the Father speaks His Logos into human flesh, He speaks everything that He has to say to humanity; all that is most precious and most dear to Him, He entrusts to us in the womb of His handmaid. He has nothing more to say about His will beyond what He brought forth in her womb and what we crucified. This is why, when we gaze into the eyes of Christ with the eyes of our heart, we begin to see things as they truly are. Under His gaze of love our prayer begins to resonate with the will of the Father.

Sacred Study and Contemplation

Although today the effort to study is reduced to the technical concerns of our contemporary academia, in Catholicism, the study of truth, sacred doctrine in particular, has been associated with prayer in various ways. For Saint Dominic they were one and the same. Mystical prayer, contemplation, and intellectual insight gained by meditation so permeate each other in the Dominican tradition that Saint Thomas Aquinas leaves the distinctions between these activities vague.

Contemplation has a wide range of meanings for Saint Thomas.[67] It can be the simple act of reasoning from one point to the next.[68] It can be an angelic vision of reality spiraling around

[67] To study, to know, to behold, to see — these are all related to contemplation. The Angelic Doctor begins to unfold these meanings in the beginning of the *Summa Theologica* when he asks whether sacred doctrine is a science (I, Q. 1, art. 2). He understands the Dominican vocation as taking up into a single way of life both contemplation and preaching (see II-II, Q. 188, arts. 5–6). Theology, or sacred doctrine, and natural theology, or what we now call philosophy of God, are complementary, the former dealing with revealed truth and the latter dealing with what can be known by nature. In formal study, we distinguish and even separate these efforts, as does Saint Thomas. He comes back to this idea again when he asks how God is known by us (I, Q. 12, arts. 5–13). In the life of prayer, it is possible that one's natural contemplation of God as manifest in what He has made dances with a consideration of what He has revealed in a manner that disposes one to the operation of the gifts of knowledge, understanding, and wisdom all at once. For more on the gifts particularly related to contemplation see *Summa Theologica* II-II, Qs. 8, 9, and 45.

[68] See his treatment of reasoning and understanding (ways we "behold" reality) as one power of the soul, in *Summa Theologica* I, Q. 79, art. 8.

itself.[69] Contemplation can also be a simple gaze that sees and appreciates the whole.[70] This activity can be simply natural or else produced under the impetus of the Holy Spirit, Who provides supernatural knowledge, understanding, and wisdom.[71]

Such mystical contemplation produces great joy and is always given for some important purpose.[72] It is not the direct result of study, but sometimes when a soul is reading Scripture or pondering a point of doctrine, it is overwhelmed with the personal presence of God. In fact, the Angelic Doctor believes that the study of sacred doctrine can occasion this kind of prayer.[73] Ancient Latin's *contemplatio* can mean to study or to read but also can refer to even higher intellectual acts produced by God.

Contemplation as Generative

In mystical contemplation, the gifts of wisdom, knowledge, and understanding move the soul in delightful ways that it does not understand. Divine light and warmth enkindle the depths of the soul and completely captivate the mind. Reason does not lead the way but is led to silent surrender with great spiritual fruitfulness. Here, the limits of human intelligence are not surmounted, but the power of reason is bowed down in adoration.

When this fire from above enkindles the mind, something is communicated that is not merely informative, but transformative. Souls baptized in this hidden radiance often wonder whether they are wasting their time. And yet, mysteriously, their

[69] Saint Thomas Aquinas, *Summa Theologica* II-II, Q. 180, art. 6.
[70] Ibid.
[71] Ibid., II-II, Qs. 8, 9, and 45.
[72] Ibid., I, Q. 43, arts. 5–6.
[73] Cf. ibid., I, Q. 1, art. 6, reply 3; II-II, Q. 43; II-II, Q. 188, art. 5.

confidence and devotion are set ablaze with a love they cannot explain. This transformation is not limited to one's life but is extended throughout one's culture and continues to extend into the future.

The saints who make this prayer their own became a source of life for others because they draw from the source of life Himself. This can happen again today for those willing to take up the discipline of withdrawing into silent adoration through what we study. Being drawn to wonder-filled silence is the beginning of spiritual maturity.

The mind is vaguely aware of everything in relation to God all at once (the gift of knowledge) and is confirmed in all manners of judgment about what God is not (the gift of understanding). These supernatural moments of understanding and knowledge mediate a transforming personal encounter with God in ways that purify and intensify our lives. The expanse and depth of these life-giving mysteries in the soul avail it to a sense of the whole (the gift of wisdom).

Entering the prayerful silence of Christian spirituality is like being lifted to a peak to gaze on vast horizons of life otherwise inaccessible to created reason. This is the complete opposite of mindlessness in prayer. Yet this conscious awareness leaves the soul in speechless adoration, humbled before the glory of divine life that shines forth in the world. The more this glory humbles us in this sacred silence, the more it generates in us and through us. According to the experts on prayerful silence and this knowledge:

> The Word proceeds from Silence, and we strive to find Him in his Source. This is because the Silence here in question is not a void or a negation but, on the contrary,

Being at Its fullest and most fruitful plenitude. That is why it generates; and that is why we keep silent.[74]

This statement is pregnant with spiritual theology, at least in its original sense as theology flowing from a living encounter with God. While some thinkers believe that progress has been made in bringing sanctity and theology together again, contemporary theology yearns to be filled with such mystical knowing.[75] This is why theologians should be men and women of prayer.

Theology is lifeless and in fact deadly if not infused by what is only born in the pregnant silence that doctrine is meant to open before us. The teachings of the Church do not explain away the mysteries of our faith; they propose them and protect them from rationalistic simplifications.

Theology, in the sense that we are considering it, is meant to have an interpersonal quality. Its study should bring us face-to-face, and heart-to-heart with a mystery above our understanding and before which we find the humility to bow our heads. It is nonetheless mindful and meaningful, in fact all the more, the more our effort to ponder God is baptized in an awareness of His presence. This kind of knowing is that which is shared by lovers, by true friends, who have suffered together and understand each other. Such knowing influences the whole theological conversation, changing the questions and providing ever-new levels to the answers.

---

[74] A Carthusian, *They Speak in Silences* (Herefordshire: Gracewing, 1955, 2006), 5–6.

[75] See Hans Urs von Balthasar, "Theology and Sanctity," in *Explorations in Theology: Word Made Flesh* (San Francisco: Ignatius Press, 1989), 181–188. This ancient notion of spiritual or mystical theology is recovered in the *Catechism of the Catholic Church* 236.

Saint Thomas gives us insight into this knowledge in his discussion on faith. In his explanation, to have faith means to believe in God, to believe what God says, and, finally, to believe for the sake of God. This third level of faith, the level of believing for the sake of God, is directional, relational, a matter of the heart.

This volitional and affective aspect to faith orients the believer to intimate friendship with God as he engages in a deeper study of his faith. As I read the Bible or ponder the insights of a Church Father, I never really enter into the text as long as I presume God to be a remote "someone" whom I merely believe exists or whom I merely trust is right about things. God is never reducible to an object of study but studies us as we study about Him. To bring faith into our study is to believe that in God is the fulfillment of all desire, even the truth that I strive to understand and suffer in the text that I read. The very form of faith, living faith, is charity — and only friendship love of God makes our study fruitful for the life of the Church and her mission to the world.

Theological Contemplation

Scientific theological conversation, committed as it is to raising insights into our faith to the highest level of human consciousness so that we can share them together, safeguards the mystical wisdom we are trying to explore but cannot fully explain it. It is not opposed to it and can even occasion it. When we inform contemplation with the doctrine of the Church, this kind of mental prayer takes on a theological quality. This theological contemplation is animated by a loving knowledge of God's presence but welcomes this presence with the understanding that the Sacred Scriptures and Holy Tradition of the Church provide.

A host of women mystics have described this deeper effort to bring doctrinal understanding and prayer together. Among these, Saint Hildegard of Bingen, Saint Teresa of Ávila, and Saint Catherine of Siena are all Doctors of the Church. We also have the writings of Blessed Elizabeth of the Trinity.

Saint Hildegard of Bingen envisioned this knowledge as an iron mountain covered with windows through which heaven gazes upon us. It is approach only through the supernatural creature of holy fear. To stand before this mountain and attend to its voice renders one vulnerable, being implicated in Christ's work of salvation and the well-being of the whole Church.

Saint Teresa of Ávila describes it as a gaze into the eyes of the One who was wounded for our sakes. It is a loving awareness of God's presence. She uses images of water, fire, and silk to convey the new life, love, and industry it establishes within.

For Catherine of Siena this knowledge is a conversation with the Father about one's life and the life of the Church. It advances by venerating His Son with kisses from His feet to His lips — the bridge from our misery to the Father's mercy. It leads to a deep plunge into the wounds of Christ for the sake of the Church.

For Elizabeth of the Trinity, this knowledge is musical. It is the praise of glory. Those who possess it are able to sing in their hearts the same song of praise Jesus offered to the Father on the Cross. It has the dimensions of redemptive and glorifying love of God and man.

All these saints are agreed that such knowledge is a sheer gift that we can fully receive only by spending time in prayer and by taking our own crosses.[76] Even after two thousand years of great saints, theologians, and mystics, theological contemplation

---

[76] Ralph Martin offers a wonderful description of this kind of knowledge in his *Fulfillment of All Desire* (Steubenville, OH: Emmaus Road, 2006), 286–304.

remains a vast, barely known frontier of human existence, for most of the inexhaustible riches of Christ are still waiting to be discovered.

This knowledge is theological contemplation, the most demanding and life changing of all human knowledge. It is mystagogical in character because it helps those who already are initiated into the life of the Church to acquire an even-deeper relationship with the Lord. The world needs Catholics to grow in this kind of contemplation.

17

A KNEELING THEOLOGY

In order to be a compelling force in social renewal, theological wisdom needs the animating power of mystical wisdom. The study of theology needs to be imbued with a deeper contemplation of the Word made flesh. Some presume that recourse to prayer in the context of theological study is anti-intellectual, a flight into fantasy, or even an escape into the merely affective. Such prejudice indicates a disconcerting shift in the nature of theological study.

Theologians of every age have striven to bring theological questions to light in a scientific and disciplined way. A scientific understanding of these questions brings them to light in the highest level of rational consciousness. Yet, for the most part, only in the modern and postmodern eras has such theological wisdom been pursued without regard for mystical wisdom.

It is time to return to a theology studied on one's knees.[77] Our greater awareness of method and recourse to technology in

---

[77] Hans Urs von Balthasar underscored the importance of a kneeling theology, a theology in which one's personal sanctity and scholarship are submitted to the sanctifying Word of God. See, for example, "Theology and Sanctity," in *Word and Redemption. Essays in Theology* 2 (New York: Herder and Herder, 1965), 49–86.

theology today seems to be at the expense of prayer. Very few scholars teach or write as if they believe that contemplation is of any objective value to the theological enterprise or that mystical wisdom has any real importance for the life of the Church. At least this is the impression one gets from what is published in many academic periodicals. Can theology without prayer build up the holiness of the Church?

Saint John of the Cross's Theological Vision

A similar problem began to raise its head in sixteenth-century Spain. Members of the Inquisition and some bishops had come to the opinion that mental prayer was dangerous. This meant that for many people throughout Spanish society, the spiritual life was limited to basic catechesis, restricted liturgical practice, recitation of vocal prayers, and the practice of moral virtue. In the meantime, many were deprived of the deeper devotion to Christ that contemplative prayer makes possible. The Carmelite Reform would be the main cultural force renewing both the Church and the broader society.

Saint John of the Cross lost his father at an early age and grew up in poverty. Through divine providence he received good schooling and had an aptitude for the liberal and fine arts, especially poetry and theology. His education grounded him in a sound humanism and understanding of the Sacred Scriptures. He loved to sing, go on hikes, camp in the wilderness, minister to the sick, and spend time in prayerful solitude.

He became a priest of considerable administrative ability. He not only helped lead the Carmelite Reform during a dangerous period, even enduring imprisonment, but he also established priories and a university. No stranger to politics, his insistence on fairness and kindness caused him to be misunderstood, rejected, and persecuted. This did not discourage the rigorous schedule of spiritual direction he maintained for priests, nuns, and the lay faithful.

To help those entrusted to his spiritual guidance, he composed beautiful poetry by which he would teach important doctrines regarding the life of prayer. In his writings there are references and explanations of what we deem to be theological contemplation, a kind of prayer that takes place deep in the heart. One of his most thought-provoking descriptions of this kind of prayer is linked to the beginning of mystical contemplation:

> O Spring like crystal!
> If only, on your silvered-over faces,
> You would suddenly form
> the eyes I have desired,
> which I bear sketched deep within my heart.[78]

This ardent prayer, this deep desire emerges in the midst of theological reflection. It represents for Saint John of the Cross a milestone in the ascent of the hidden mountain and entrance into the secret garden of contemplation. We have already seen how he begins the *Spiritual Canticle* by describing a spiritual awakening in terms of an ardent lover pleading with her beloved to show himself. From this John of the Cross goes on to describe the journey of a soul searching for Christ in terms of the messengers He sends and the enemies that must be faced. Here, he takes us to the threshold of a deeper encounter, a tender face-to-face, a reflection on sacred doctrine that leads to a more mature union with God.

---

[78] Saint John of the Cross, *Spiritual Canticle*, stanza 12, in *Complete Works*, 515.

FIRE FROM ABOVE

Sacred Doctrine as a Living Fount for Prayer

The soul who withdraws to seek God dwelling in its depths contains a fountain of living water according to Saint John of the Cross. This image speaks to the beauty of the truths of the faith received into the heart. They have the quality of water, which in stillness becomes smooth. The more fully sacred doctrine is received into one's life, the smoother or more peaceful theology becomes to reflect on.

Beyond a simple mental assent to theological facts, receiving these teachings means to allow them to pierce our dull indifference so that we might treasure them as a gift from a friend. How we treat the gift reveals our attitude toward the giver. Applying oneself to the study of sacred doctrine with grateful devotion purifies and strengthens our faith. Saint John of the Cross is describing this inner purity when he speaks about the surface of these waters being smooth like crystal and as reflective as silver.[79]

What is sought in this reflection and how it is sought constitutes the essential character of theological contemplation. One who is deeply in love thinks about her beloved all the time and, when he cannot be found, yearns to glimpse his eyes in every reflection. Those who ponder the truths of our faith filled with longing for Christ yearn for them to yield a sign of His presence.[80]

---

[79] Saint Thomas Aquinas explains this purifying effect of contemplation in terms of the operation of the infused gifts of knowledge, understanding, and wisdom. *Summa Theologica* II-II, Qs. 8, 9, and 45.

[80] Saint John of the Cross, *Spiritual Canticle* 12:5 and 13:2, in *Complete Works*, 517–520. Saint John Paul II, in his doctoral dissertation at the Angelicum, explains that the description of the Lord's presence in doctrine is noteworthy because "it stimulates a vehement desire to see." *Faith according to Saint John of the Cross,*

The Reflective Quality
of Sacred Doctrine

The reflective quality of the water describes an essential characteristic of the sacred doctrine that waters the heart. Saint
Thomas Aquinas says that the articles of faith are truth bearing:
they bear relation to the First Truth, who is God.[81] Saint John of
the Cross brings this insight to bear on Saint Paul's description
that we "see" by faith "dimly" as in "a mirror" (see 1 Cor. 3:12).
In the Carmelite's description of the role of sacred doctrine in
prayer, faith finds the revelation of Truth Himself reflected in
the articles of the faith as in a mirror.

Saint John of the Cross's teaching helps explain the enthusiasm we witnessed in Denver during the liturgies of World Youth
Day, '93. There is a relation that the sacred doctrine of our faith
bears to the presence of the Lord. The Lord's presence is accessible to us in propositions of our faith, not with the clarity
provided by our natural power of understanding, but obscurely,
dimly as if in a reflection.

Sacred doctrine is essential for the spiritual life because it
makes it possible to gaze on Christ Himself. The more we study
the faith with devotion of heart, the more we expose ourselves
to wonder and awe before the Lord. Over and above what we
understand theologically, prayerful reflection on what we believe

---

trans. Jordan Aumann (San Francisco: Ignatius Press, 1981, repr.
1985, 1986), 210. Theological contemplation is nothing other
than a gaze into doctrine motivated by this desire.

[81] See Saint Thomas Aquinas, *Summa Theologica* II-II, Q. 1, art. 1.
Probably the most compelling explanation of this is that provided by Romanus Cessario, *The Virtue of Faith and the Theological
Life* (Washington, DC: Catholic University of America Press,
1996), 63–76.

gives a loving general knowledge of Him in a personal and intimate manner.

The "eyes" of the Lord formed in this reflection stir intense desires in the heart, according to the Carmelite Master. In other words, it is possible to be deeply moved, profoundly shaken when in our efforts to ponder our faith we catch the Lord's piercing love reflected in them. Saint John describes this presence of Christ as no less than "remarkable." [82] Sacred doctrine, far from remaining on the level of abstract speculation, reflects the gaze of Someone who looks on us with love. When "sketched deep within" the heart, this kind of knowledge occasions spiritual maturity. [83]

---

[82] Saint John of the Cross, *Spiritual Canticle* 12:5, in *Complete Works*, 517.

[83] Ibid., 12:6, in *Complete Works*, 517. "Sketched" is contrasted with a completed painting in this passage, as a way of describing how this kind of knowledge is not yet beatific vision, but an anticipation of it, something that will come to completion when we pass out of the light of faith given in this life into the light of glory offered in the next. This experience, this knowledge, in the context of the poem, causes a soul to move from the yearning but unsettled desires with which one begins the spiritual life into a more peaceful and confident friendship love—qualities that indicate proficiency in following the Lord.

18

THE CONFRONTATION OF PRAYER AND DOUBT

We have already discussed the silence of God when we proposed obedience as an essential moment in our conversation with God. We suggested that when God seems most absent, our obedience purifies and intensifies our faith. For this to happen, the obedience we offer in mental prayer must be directed to a deeper love of God, a deeper devotion to Him, a deeper bond between His will and ours.

At this point in our conversation, however, we need to revisit this discussion to address a legitimate concern about whether people of prayer should also be people who think. In the history of mystical contemplation, some have charged the great mystics with a certain kind of obscurantism. This approach to truth, they charge, opposes human progress.

In the United States, the sociologist Robert Merton was very concerned that education be freed from an approach that emphasized obedience and contemplation. Following leading German scientists, he believed that the obedience that contemplation requires was opposed to the freedom that students need for scholarly inquiry. This kind of contemplation, he charged, was an obstacle to scientific understanding. These are false dichotomies but they have influenced the way many understand contemplation and the obedience of faith that goes with it.

When, for example, John of the Cross speaks of the importance of "dark" contemplation, some misunderstand this to mean that mystical prayer means accepting obscurity for obscurity's sake. Mystical knowledge is on the level of the religious imagination and pious feelings but is not actually a real form of knowing. This is not exactly what Saint John of the Cross intended.

Mystical knowledge is not opposed to enlightenment — just distinct from every natural form of it. Sometimes natural forms of enlightenment can be concomitant with mystical wisdom, but they are not essential to it. True, a particular contemplative might lack a certain practical know-how but still be very saintly. Yet someone who is clever at prudential judgment can also be a great mystic.

Saint John of the Cross was a brilliant poet and literary master, but he also understood that his poetry and command over the humanities of his time did not in themselves lead to union with God. Contemplation in faith remained the only sure path for which he would argue. At the same time, he used his poetry and love for language to advance contemplation in faith. He did not see education or study as an obstacle, but he did understand that the satisfaction that we take in it needs to be subordinated to more sublime forms of knowledge.

Living by Evidence of What Is Not Seen

Faith is the evidence of things not seen.[84] This does not mean that our faith is meaningless or that to pray is to plunge into

[84] Heb. 11:1. See also Saint Thomas Aquinas, *Summa Theologica* II-II, Q. 4, art. 1.

nihilism. To have this evidence of what is invisible, of what is spiritual, is to have received a gift from above. Our natural powers of understanding cannot find this ground on their own. We must learn not to rely on what seems so clear to us, because, in this life, union with God is something that we do not directly know with clarity, but only dimly, as if reflected through a mirror.

This is especially true when the Lord seems absent or when our prayers seem not to be answered. In times of great stress and crisis, a consoling thought or spiritual feeling is not enough. When we are overwhelmed by shock and simply do not know how to respond, avoiding the situation or cleverly surmounting it is not always possible. We must learn how to bring these difficult ambiguities into our conversation with the Lord.

For Saint John of the Cross, these moments are not obstacles to our life of faith but are opportunities in which a new kind of mystical knowledge can more securely flow into our faith.[85] To help us reach union with God quickly, Saint John of the Cross invites us to confront these doubts with prayer and search them with faith. Instead of trying to find an answer or make sense out of the hardship, the powers of our natural intelligence must allow themselves to be bathed in God's divine splendor.

This is a simple movement of trust and love. The mysterious heat and light that shine through this kind of faith is like a radiant sun. The brightness of God in the darkness of faith overshadows, purifies, and opens the eyes of the soul.[86]

To enter into union with God, we do not seek what can be understood or felt or imagined in our prayer. Instead, in those ambiguous and difficult spaces in our lives, God is speaking in

---

[85] See Saint John of the Cross, *Dark Night of the Soul* 2:16:9.
[86] See Saint John of the Cross, *Ascent of Mount Carmel* 2:4:6.

His own language directly into our hearts. This language of love surpasses our ability to feel or intuit or know or understand, but what we do not understand in the secrets that the Lord entrusts to us is essential for leading us to union with God. This secret wisdom purifies and intensifies our humanity more than the sum total of everything that we might understand, imagine, or feel in prayer.

God Himself is the only real consolation, and only He can provide an understanding—but the solid ground that He invites us to stand on is beyond our natural powers to grasp. It is humbly given from above, and we receive it in humility. The ground on which He establishes us is none other than that of Calvary. What He reveals silences all attempts to understand. To stand with Him in this supreme moment of prayer, regardless of what we feel, answers everything.

This is why what we experience in Christian contemplation is very different from what we expect or what we think we need. The reality of heaven is cloaked in painful ambiguity in this life, and faith does not take away the ambiguity, not completely and not in the way that we want it to. We want clear answers and consoling reassurances. Instead, in the midst of intense anxiety and anguish, we are not given clear answers. Instead, we sit through hours of painful questions and patiently learn how to surrender each of these to God.

The Fullness Conveyed in Divine Silence

In His mysterious silence in prayer, God is communicating in a more wonderful way. When things seem to have gone completely wrong and all our plans have run amiss, He whispers a truly wonderful secret, something from the depths of His Heart into the depths of ours. Prayer has the power to bring faith into every doubt and difficulty. Such conversation with God sanctifies these difficult ambiguities when they compel us to seek by faith what we cannot see by reason.

In difficult doubts, we are awaited by the mysterious knowledge of the glory of God in the face of Christ (see 2 Cor. 4:6, 18). This kind of knowledge feels more like unknowing than knowing. This is mystical knowledge. The soul that possesses this finds less satisfaction in what it understands about the faith than in what it does not understand: the ineffable incomprehensibility of Divine Love. This is the bosom of the Trinity:

> What peace, what love, what silence is in that divine bosom! How lofty the science God teaches there, the anagogical acts that so enkindle the heart.[87]

"Anagogical acts" refers to a hidden, secret knowing of God's presence. This supernatural cognition is more like unknowing than what we usually call knowing, because it does not leave the heart with the satisfaction of having figured something out. Instead, the soul is confounded. It does not know or experience that it is completely bathed in wonder. It is not even aware that it is bathed in anything at all, but can feel lost, abandoned, wondering whether it is wasting its time, suspicious that it has done something wrong.

This is the beginning of heaven in faith. Eternity for creatures born in time is unfamiliar. The crashing in of heaven's glory is not comfortable. Even for souls who are completely purified, this illumination remains something completely unknown to itself. This is why having a spiritual director is so important the more we grow in prayer. In what seems to be complete emptiness and without any meaning, the wisdom of another can help us to hold firm to that hidden glory secretly at work within.

---

[87] See Saint John of the Cross, *Sayings of Light and Love*, no. 139.

Time spent in this silent theological contemplation makes space for humility before this mystery of God in daily life. Resting in this loving knowledge, assenting to it, allowing it to pierce the heart, sanctifies misfortune and constantly endows new eternal meaning to all of life's seemingly accidental mishaps. This is not because the ambiguity is diminished, but because, in the ambiguity, God's unfamiliar clarity shines through. He is present over the chaos, bringing light that cannot be overcome by the darkness. Only such a spiritual knowledge rooted in adoration of God can save and build up humanity.

God's Mysterious Absence in Deep Prayer

Contemplation does not shield us from doubt or suffering. Christian prayer baptizes our doubts and difficulties, trials and tests in faith. Violently opposing forces, faith confronts doubt in prayer even in the midst of very difficult circumstances.

Saint Thérèse of Lisieux lived a life of intense prayer and friendship with the Lord. In the last weeks of her short life, after suffering for more than a year from tuberculosis, she was ordered to finish her autobiography. It was during this suffering that she began to understand that there were people who had lost their faith. This insight moved her with deep compassion:

> Although I would not have believed it before, Jesus has given me a sense that there really are souls without faith. Through an abuse of grace, they have lost the true joy that comes from this priceless treasure.[88]

Until these final months of her life, she was completely mystified by believers who once had this gift but had lost it. She

---

[88] Saint Thérèse of Lisieux, *The Story of a Soul*, chap. 10.

simply presumed everyone knew the joy that she found in her faith. Why would they not do everything possible to try to get it back? Now in her terminal illness, God helps her question this presumption.

By doing so, He is implicating her in His work of mercy. Mercy suffers the misery of others to relieve their pain and restore their sense of dignity. To this end, the Lord communicates a difficult and unfamiliar message:

> He allowed a thick darkness to invade my spirit. The very thought of heaven, previously a consolation, became the source of struggle and torment.

The Lord wants her to understand what those who do not know Him suffer. This means that He allows her to suffer the absence of the joy of our faith. Thus the consolation of certain doctrines, such as the doctrine of heaven, is no longer something that she experiences in prayer. The Lord continued to communicate to her by this absence of joy to her last life's breath:

> This trial was to last more than a few days or a few weeks. It would continue until the hour set by God Himself. This hour has not yet come.[89]

God permits the absence of joy only for an important reason. He does not withhold a blessing unless to give us a greater blessing. In order to understand the absence of joy that Saint Thérèse suffered, it is helpful to consider the greater blessing that the Lord was giving her.

She writes about a spiritual joy she finds in the midst of her suffering. The suffering she writes about is not merely a physical

[89] Ibid.

experience, but above all a spiritual trial. From her experience, we can understand that spiritual joy is not due to the absence of spiritual suffering. Instead, this joy from above is found in the midst of a suffering her spirit endures here below.

It is important to note that in the Christian life of prayer, spiritual maturity does not consist in an absence of suffering. In this life, the more we love, the more we suffer—physically, psychologically, and above all spiritually. Real love is not limited by the merely convenient. It costs. For the one who loves, however, whatever the sacrifice, it is always too little.

When love costs nothing, it does not mean very much. Without suffering, love risks being no more than a sentimental thought or a good intention. What it costs helps us see what the love actually means. Suffering patiently all kinds of difficulties for the Lord and for others proves our love and makes it real.

The reason this darkness was a particular trial for Saint Thérèse was that in the past, when suffering difficult times, she was able to sustain herself by entering into deep prayer and resting in the thought of heaven. Now the thought of heaven was almost impossible to bear.

It was not that she did not believe in heaven. She held it as a matter of faith. But her own personal relationship with what she believed left her in torment. She simply could not believe that she could be happy in the heaven that she professed. Whatever light this belief offered was withheld from her. Just what beatitude really was, as opposed to what she imagined it to be, seems to have deeply troubled her spirit.

Offering It Up

To live by faith means to be faithful to God even when our feelings, our thoughts, and our imagination cannot find Him.

This trial of spiritual darkness is so overbearing that we can feel tempted to doubt, to forsake our life of faith. Yet suffering this darkness that causes people to doubt is not the same as doubting. Instead, if we choose to believe in the merciful love of God anyway, we make of even this suffering a powerful sacrifice of praise.

What is the difference between doubt and suffering the lack of joy doubt causes? Faith. When we believe in the love of God even when we do not feel it, we are exercising our faith. When we lift our hearts in prayer even when God does not seem to be there, our prayer is all the more precious to Him. He sees the sacrifice, and He understands the cost.

Jesus Himself did not brush over our human experience during His Passion and death. He fully entered into it — enjoying and suffering to the last drop everything about our life in this world, except sin itself. Although He never doubted, He did share with us the sometimes dehumanizing anguish that doubt can engender in those who love or want to love God.

Jesus prayed Psalm 22 as he struggled to breathe on the Cross. This is a prayer of a man tormented by his enemies, rejected by society, tortured, and left to die in humiliation. Although it ultimately becomes a prayer of confidence in God, the psalm begins with a crucified man's agonizing question to God: "Why have you abandoned me?"

By saving us in this way, even to the point of bearing the suffering of doubt, Jesus opens all of human experience, including doubt, to the mercy of God. If doubts oppress us and make prayer difficult, we do not suffer this alone. The Lord has entered this experience too.

Darkness is an ordeal but not a sin. Doubt, on the other hand, is a choice. Ordeals are given us to help us grow and to make our love for God and one another more meaningful, more beautiful.

When, in the face of difficult darkness, we renounce doubt and choose to believe in God's love, our faith becomes strong and so does our ability to pray.

Christians can suffer the darkness of doubt even if they do not choose to doubt but instead choose to believe. The extent to which Christ has already suffered this same darkness is revealed on the Cross. He has descended into our darkest experiences so that we would not suffer alone, so that in looking at Him, we might recover our dignity. If we also confront this darkness, we do not do so alone. He is with us. By faith, even this darkness of doubt can become a way to share in Christ's salvific mission.

This means that if anyone is struggling with such darkness in his life, it is still possible to believe even in the face of such overbearing difficulty. It is simply a matter of crying out with faith in prayer. It is a matter of asking and begging God for the strength to persevere in love in the midst of this trial. When we choose to believe in spite of such darkness, when we raise our hearts in prayer even when it feels as if there is no reason to do so, this is when we are in special solidarity with the Lord.

The Great Offering of the Little Flower

Saint Thérèse, in fact, before she received this trial, had asked Jesus to use her in a special way to extend His mercy to those who most needed it. To answer such a beautiful petition, to allow her to help extend the mercy of God to those who most needed it, the Lord would need to allow Thérèse to share in the darkness that afflicted those furthest from Him. Today, thousands upon thousands have found support in their own struggles with doubt through the prayer she learned to offer to God.

Under the crushing logic of doubt, those who do not believe do not know the joy of Christian hope and feel pressed by a banal meaninglessness. In solidarity with them, Thérèse confronted in her heart this overwhelming effect of doubt even as she battled to believe. Our Christian faith did not take her away from the ambiguities and inner drama of those who do not believe. It inserted her more deeply into it.

As she faced her terminal illness, she entered into the battle of faith, the contest against doubt that is won only through prayer. Struggling to believe in the love of God, she learned on a much deeper level to beg for mercy for herself. More than that, she learned to intercede for the mercy of God on those whose misery she shared.

Her prayer entered into the depths of a deeper love, a more encompassing compassion. God allowed her to suffer such an intense struggle with doubt because of the immeasurable good that prayer can do when the love with which we pray is purified and deepened. Only through suffering all kinds of trials and hardships is the love with which we pray made perfect.

This is the thing about suffering anything for God's sake: the greater the love with which our sacrifices are offered, the greater the space in our hearts for God's power to be unleashed in the world. Spiritual space in the heart is the capacity to give God the freedom to move in us and act in us with His saving love. Giving God this freedom requires that we die to ourselves sometimes in regards to very good things.

Saint Thérèse was moved to surrender even the joy that the thought of heaven once gave her so that God's love could teach her compassion for those who did not believe in anything beyond this life. In doing this, she gave God space, the freedom to give something even greater than the fleeting joy the thought of heaven can give. Her suffering allowed the joy of heaven to enter the world in better ways.

To accept such a cross is to participate in Christ's work of redemption. Such participation is possible because the mystery of the Cross is superabundant with vast spaces for our own works of love to extend their power in cooperation with Him. Because prayer opens the heart to this freedom of Christ, it is decisive for confronting doubt with faith.

The experience of Saint Thérèse of Lisieux invites us to consider how those who join themselves to Christ by faith are invited by Him to share in this saving mission, to bear the misery that afflicts those who have, to varying degrees, rejected God. If we begin prayer feeling as if we are afflicted with painful doubts and difficulties, we must ask how we have abused the graces richly bestowed on us. We must also ask what it is that Christ is entrusting to us now, what it is that He is asking us to bear with Him.

Mercy is love that suffers the misery of another in such a way that the person's dignity is affirmed. Jesus, by sharing the suffering that our doubts cause, has transformed this anguish into a kind of spiritual place where we can discover His presence. He is with you in this experience, ready to protect you and give you the strength you need to get through it.

19

MYSTICAL WISDOM: FIRE FROM ABOVE

One descends this pathway of self-knowledge by a silent attentiveness to the Lord. In this effort to pray, we collect the powers
of our soul and concentrate them on our awareness of the Lord's
presence with us. Our intellect, our imagination, our memory,
even our feelings are united in a silent, gentle, loving awareness
in faith that He is present. This kind of prayer is called holy
recollection.

In this prayer, we are wholly vigilant for Christ as we descend
into the absence of love in the heart. We can encounter in this
descent all kinds of darkness, sorrow, and pain. Sometimes we
become aware of painful memories of failing others or of others
who have failed us. In holy recollection, our spirit questions
these experiences and asks, "How is the Lord present in this
sorrow, this inadequacy, this void?"

Recollection does not seek easy answers. It seeks faith. We
draw our powers together not to "figure out" what God is doing
but instead "to believe" that no matter what has happened or
what we have done, He is present and at work. Whether we are
fully aware of these voids and inadequacies or not, they dispose
us to all kinds of rash judgment and impatience as long as we do

not believe that the merciful love of the Lord is present in them somehow. Yet by becoming aware of these wounds of sin in the presence of the Lord, we can begin to surrender them to Him. He is present to make this spiritual burden light.

The slope of holy recollection slides into this abyss of misery not for the sake of self-pity, but to search for Christ. It is not a time for self-absorption or an excessive examination of our motives. The heart is a twisted and dark labyrinth if we enter it without faith in God. With the presence of God, we discover in the abyss of our misery the even greater abyss of His mercy.

We are not alone; we are loved and cherished. We do not suffer alone; the Lord suffers with us. This is true no matter what we have done or what has happened to us. We have not been forgotten or abandoned. We are remembered, and God has implicated Himself in our plight. Our lives are not meaningless. Our lives count. No life is a mistake. Each and every life is part of an exquisite plan of unfathomable goodness. We are desired and unimaginably loved by God.

Each unique person is created with unfathomable value and eternal worth. Each one of us is created unique and treasured uniquely by God. God is always with us, always for us. His heart aches over the heartaches we suffer. He suffers with us what we lack in our hearts. He is waiting for us to turn to Him and rely on His power in our weakness. Holy recollection constantly discovers new, beautiful ways in which we are awaited by Merciful Love.

As Blessed Elizabeth of the Trinity turned to prayer, she was overwhelmed by the Lord's presence in her misery: bearing her up, suffering her lack of love with her, and restoring her dignity. Borrowing language from other mystics, she called this encounter with God's mercy in her misery the divine impact.[90] Her misery was limited by God's mercy, just as a weaker force is contained by a more powerful impulse.

In prayer, she discovered the surging sea of Divine Love crashing in on her emptiness. In the face of the immensity of God's overwhelming love, she was able to let go of her old way of life, including her fiery temper. Her lack of gentleness suffered a mystical death that God's gentleness might begin to reign. In prayer she discovered a mortification of her irrational inner impulses by which she might live by love.

After she became a Carmelite nun, she was convinced that this encounter of the Lord in the heart was essential not only for priests and religious but also for the lay faithful. She wrote a retreat in which she counsels her married sister, a mother of young children: "The divine impact occurs in the deepest depths, where the abyss of our nothingness touches the Abyss of mercy, the whole totality of God's immensity. There we will find strength to die to ourselves and, losing all vestige of self, we will be changed into love."[91]

Seeking God in nothingness as Elizabeth describes rings with primordial overtones of creation. Prayer takes on the proportions of a new creation, in which the chaotic vestiges of a self alienated from God are lost and a new identity rooted in the very reality of God is established. The all of God, the totality of His immensity, is known in the human heart through encountering Divine Mercy. The search for the Lord within is the effort to find those places in the substance of the soul where God's mercy and human misery touch each other, where one has bearing on the other.

---

[90] See, for example, her Letter 335 to Sr. Marie-Odile.
[91] See Blessed Elizabeth of the Trinity, *Heaven in Faith*, no. 5.

Habitare Secum — Living within Oneself

Is it really important to consider our nothingness when we look for the Lord's merciful presence in our lives? Those who seek the presence of the Lord in the dark places of their hearts learn the secret of *habitare secum*, the secret of living with oneself.[92] There are such dark places in our lives; only with the mercy of the Lord can we face ourselves and deal with the reality of who we are.

This ideal began to be articulated around the time of Saint Benedict, although it was a lived part of Christian spirituality from the very beginning. It means not only confessing sin and doing penance for the evil that we have done, but also accepting our weaknesses and learning to offer our limitations to God. Most especially, *habitare secum* means being able to enter into the depths of our hearts to listen humbly to the Lord, who waits for us there.

Christian prayer deals with the reality of the human heart. The heart is the spring from which flows good and evil. It is broken and wounded, laden with many sorrows, and yet still capable of finding joy in what is good. It is an inner sanctuary where God speaks to us. People who do not want to deal with themselves or deal with God do not like to go there. They remain unfamiliar to themselves and unaware of what is driving them in life. Yet, when God calls us to Himself and we begin to yearn to be with

---

[92] Like other ideas in the Rule of Saint Benedict, *habitare secum* is not easily translated. The concept is closely tied with the pledge of conversatio morum, which comes up in the same paragraph. Before one joins the community by pledging obedience, stability, and ongoing conversion (conversatio morum), a candidate is to spend some time being tested, learning the Rule, and living with himself (habitare secum). See Rule of Saint Benedict, no. 58.

Him, the best ways to find Him are by entering into our hearts, accepting what is there, and offering it to the Lord.

The reason for this has to do with the theme of mercy in Pope Benedict XVI's homily at the beatification of John Paul II. John Paul II had said that mercy is the limit of evil. He loved the theme of Divine Mercy. It was the mercy of God that helped him deal with the cruel brutality of World War II, which was followed by decades of Soviet oppression.

Saint John Paul was convinced that Divine Mercy is the limit of evil because the more he trusted in Jesus, the more he saw the triumph of mercy. Contemplating the face of Christ and clinging to the mercy of God was the secret not only of dealing with himself but also of being merciful to others, even those who tried to kill him. His confidence in Divine Mercy made John Paul II a compelling advocate for the dignity of the human person, which is why people all over the world were drawn to him.

Evil, the mystery of sin, dehumanizes, but Divine Mercy raises on high! Mercy is love that suffers the misery of another, the evil that afflicts someone's heart, so that the dignity of that person might be restored. On the Cross, Christ embraced our misery so that we might know God's mercy.

The good and evil we find in the heart there are *not* coequal principles, because good has definitively triumphed over evil in the death and Resurrection of Jesus Christ. When we turn to Him in faith, He gives us the power of His mercy and teaches us to realize the victory of good over evil in our lives. He has already suffered our misery with us and is ever ready to meet us there; so that in Him all that is good, noble, and true about us is rescued from the mystery of sin and raised to new life.

To learn to live with ourselves — this is to look at those places in our lives where evil has a foothold, offering them to God so that we can realize in ourselves how Divine Mercy is the limit of evil. If the abyss of our misery is deep, the abyss of mercy is inexhaustibly deeper: the One crucified by love bears with us the absence of love, the misery, with which we are afflicted so that, by our union with His suffering, we are constantly more deeply established in His love — a love that surpasses every sin, limitation, privation, failure, and weakness.

The more we discover this limit to the evil in our own hearts, the more we can rejoice in the remarkable and astonishing presence of the Lord in our lives. Rather than being driven by all kinds of brokenness we do not understand, we find ourselves able to live like Saint Benedict, Saint John Paul II, and the other great saints who, through such interior deliberation, discovered the secret of living with themselves before the face of God. Habitare secum is an interior search for the Mercy of the Lord.

Dryness in Prayer

Saint Teresa explains that we should expect aridity, dislike, and distaste for prayer in the beginning. Sometimes, even the very advanced go through these experiences. This is like lowering the bucket into the well and appearing to pull it up empty. When hard work seems to bear no fruit, Saint Teresa advises that our efforts are not in vain. She admonishes us to keep our eyes focused confidently on the Lord of the Garden, even when we are utterly exhausted in prayer. Our tears are not as pleasing to the Lord as are our effort and our humility.

After describing beginning to pray as drawing up water from a well, Saint Teresa goes on to explain the prayer of quiet and other kinds of contemplation. A few comments on the prayer of quiet will help us put into context the initial struggles and frustrations that afflict us, so that we will be able to begin with more patience and hope. Teresa explains that prayer becomes easier as we acquire the habit of recollection. Indeed, we become more comfortable not only with God but also with ourselves. The ancient practice of habitare secum informs our existence. Being at peace with ourselves to a minimal degree, we begin to experience better self-control and awareness of the sweetness of God.

To describe how this kind of prayer is different from the simple efforts we make to meditate on Christ or our efforts to search for Christ hidden in the difficult parts of our lives, Saint Teresa uses the image of a windlass pumping water. When we first begin to pray, we water our garden by first drawing water with a bucket. That is, we work hard to think about the Lord and what He has done for us. This effort can be exhausting and tedious at first. The problem is that we are not sure what we want. The Lord attracts us, but our heart is still divided. But after a time of drawing the refreshing water of Christ, we become more and more confident about what we really want. The powers of our soul begin to coalesce around Him.

Once the habit of prayerfulness is formed in us, rather than pulling water out of a well with a bucket, it is as if we have a spiritual hand pump drawing devotion from our hearts. Some mistake this recollection for a detached self-satisfied mental state that escapes into a disingenuous piety and sits in judgment over everyone else. Real recollection does not admit of such aggression. On the contrary, the heart habitually recollected in quiet prayerfulness and submitting itself to the voice of Christ is sober, humble, and deeply compassionate.

Those who have learned to recollect their powers in the Lord suffer from hunger and thirst for spiritual things, and long for the peace that only the Lord can give. They do not feel worthy of the Lord's love, and yet their thoughts are always turned toward Him. They are compassionate toward the suffering and weaknesses of others, and their ardent desire for the Lord does not allow them to be as judgmental as they once were. Less divided in their desires and more focused on Jesus, the prayerfully recollected constantly seek more silence in their lives and ache for Him all the time.

The Beginning of Mystical Prayer

All Christian prayer is mystical insofar as it is a vital part of our union with the mystery of Christ, through the holy mysteries or sacraments of the Church, for the sake of unity with the Mystery of the Holy Trinity. This mystical life makes progress by means of the Cross. Likewise, contemplative prayer develops as an ever more profound participation in Christ's suffering and death. Growth in contemplative prayer helps us make of ourselves a more complete spiritual offering to God in the pattern of Christ.

When considered from the standpoint of grace, contemplative prayer admits of ascetical and mystical degrees. Ascetical degrees of prayer denote proficiency in spiritual exercises that are acquired by practice. Cooperating with the graces God gives for this, a soul can acquire a certain prayerful awareness and attitude. The practices of meditation and recollection speak to this grace-filled awareness and attitude.

Yet virtues and enlightenment attained under our own natural impetus do not delineate the height or depth of prayer. In addition to graces we freely cooperate with, there are also graces at work that surpass our natural operations. These infused graces operate under the impetus of the Holy Spirit insofar as we sanction them and allow them to work. Prayer progresses by means of these infused graces with a fruitfulness and union with Christ that our natural activity, even when aided by grace, could never achieve.

As the flowers in our garden begin to grow, Saint Teresa speaks of this more refreshing kind of prayer. It does not involve the same amount of labor. Rather than our having to draw water from a well, devotion flows through this kind of prayer as if by a canal system or by means of free-falling rain showers.

In this prayer, the Lord captures our hearts with the fire of His love. This fire is first of all the gift of the Holy Spirit. The more the Holy Spirit is at work in our souls, the more He communicates the Truth who is Christ and the more ardent He makes our love for the Lord. His love inflames our love until it is difficult to discern where one ends and the other begins. At first, this love is just a little spark, but it is a divine spark that can ignite a raging fire.

How does this fire of God's love ignite our prayer? On a natural level, when we deeply love someone, we cannot be at peace until we are with that person. Then, when we finally enjoy the person's company, the more we are with him, the deeper we feel at peace. This rule of love applies in a special way to God.

As the feelings of devotion that come from the Holy Spirit flow in deeper and more intense ways, the spark of mystical prayer grows into a flame, and this flame, if safeguarded by a disciplined life, roars into a blazing fire. The point is that contemplative prayer opens us up to God's love in beautiful ways. Our perseverance and determination create an environment in our hearts where He is free to work.

There is one final observation for a correct understanding of Saint Teresa's degrees of prayer. Even though there is a certain progress from one kind of prayer to another, it should not be assumed that mystical contemplation is given only to those who have mastered meditation and recollection. Neither is it limited to the spiritually mature. Someone can be very immature and doctrinally ill formed and still be lifted up by infused graces of contemplation.

Saint Teresa was surprised and even concerned by this. Advanced experiences in prayer or extraordinary phenomena were not reliable signs of spiritual maturity. The Lord seemed to give different experiences of prayer whenever and to whomever He chose, and He did so regardless of apparent unworthiness or immaturity. That a soul should experience such graces is much more an indication of God's faithfulness to the soul than of the soul's faithfulness to Him.

Saint Teresa even found herself taken deep into mystical prayer when she was not fully recollected. When she was assailed by all kinds of distracting thoughts and unworthy fantasies, the Lord continued to burn in her heart like a steady candle. Sometimes, when she thought herself furthest from Him, His love would flash out like flame, giving her beautiful insight and deep spiritual affections.

Meditation and recollected silence can dispose to mystical contemplation, but they are not required for it. Not even feelings of devotion or tears of compunction are required. This is because in this higher form of prayer the Holy Spirit is praying in us. Sometimes He also moves our intellect, imagination, and emotions. He is, however, sovereign to move how and where He wills. All the Lord needs is our ardent effort to be faithful, to cleave to Him by living faith. He is ever ready to do His part when we make the least bit of effort to do ours.

20

THE ROLE OF MARY IN
MENTAL PRAYER

Popular devotion is very important for contemplative prayer.
Holy images, beautiful churches, holy shrines, rosaries, and Eucharistic Adoration are given to us to dispose us to a deeper
encounter with God. Mary is of special importance. In fact, at
the threshold of a Carthusian's cell is an image to our Lady before
which he asks for her intercession whenever he enters or leaves.

Different cultures have developed different expressions of
Marian piety. These sources of contemplative prayer need to be
rediscovered and promoted now more than ever. In particular,
devotions to our Lady are especially necessary in the hypermas-
culinized world in which we live. Her witness to maternal love
and obedience to God keeps before us all that is good, noble,
and true about the gift of our humanity.

In Mary, the mystery of woman lives at the heart of the
Church. Because of the wonder of her faith, she is the icon of
what the whole ecclesial reality means. Different forms of popular
devotion can deepen this relationship so that, together with His
Mother, we might more deeply love the Lord. This chapter is
dedicated to promoting a more lively devotion to Mary as an
aid for growth in Christian contemplation and mystical wisdom.

The Witness of Saint John Paul II

John Paul II discovered the secret of making a new beginning daily as a young man in Krakow at the time of the Nazi invasion. His parish was administered by Salesian priests who knew that their days were numbered. In fact, many Polish priests would be interned in concentration camps during the war, and a significant number of these would die in the midst of the most brutal conditions. The Salesians prepared for this eventuality by asking a layman to form a prayer group of young people who would be trained in the spiritual life and catechesis. The prayer group was called the Living Rosary. Each member would form his own Living Rosary group so that when the priests were imprisoned, the faith could continue.

The layman whom they tapped was a tailor noted for his deep prayer and knowledge of Saint John of the Cross. Jan Tyranowski had chosen his life of solitude and his humble occupation because it provided him the silence he needed to enter into deep prayer. At the same time, although he was simple, he was not a simpleton. Rather, he was an intellectual whose understanding of spiritual theology introduced the young people entrusted to him to deep truths regarding the human person and the nature of faith. Saint John Paul II's approach in his doctoral studies on Saint John of the Cross suggests an originality that might have been born in the catechesis providing through Tyranowski's Living Rosary catechesis.

Besides the Carmelite doctrine on prayer and spiritual growth, to which much of this book has been dedicated, another important part of the catechesis Tyranowski offered in the spiritual life is the maternal role of Mary in the life of prayer. Because of her unique relationship with Christ, she has a special role to play in the spiritual life of each believer. Her prayer for us helps us in our efforts to pray. Tyranowski advocated that those who love Jesus should take His Mother into their homes.

At the end of the last hour of the liturgical day, Night Prayer, the Church commends everything to the intercession of the Virgin Mary. She is a special protection through the night until the new day. So too, as we come to the end of this work, do we commend ourselves to the Lord's Mother, who is solicitous that we should always "do whatever he tells you" (John 2:5).

Marian Consecration

John Paul II would eventually consecrate himself to Mary according to the form proposed by Saint Louis de Montfort, a great mystic whose teaching is deeply rooted in what many call the French School of spirituality. Key to this teaching is that growth in holiness is realized through a special kind of identification with Jesus through Mary.

This identification does not designate the absorption or destruction of one's unique individuality by a smothering nonpersonal pantheistic reality. Accepting the gift of Mary disposes us instead to a relational mysticism. It proposes a pathway by which we let go of our own projects and self-serving enterprises and choose to live for Christ in service to others.

The Lord's gift of His Mother to us is vital to this kind of participation in His work of redemption. By embracing her special relation to Him as Mother in our life of prayer, our own relation to God and to one another is rendered more vulnerable to sharing in the life of grace that Christ came to give us. We accept and embrace the spiritual gift of the Lord's Mother in our lives when we consecrate ourselves to Jesus through Mary.

Saint John Paul II personally experienced how authentic devotion to Mary leads to deeper union with Jesus. When he was a very young boy, his own mother died. His father understood this crushing sorrow. He took young Karol with him on a pilgrimage from their hometown of Wadowice to Kalwaria, a sanctuary in the foothills designed as a replica of holy sites of Jerusalem. In the main church, Karol was entrusted to Our Lady of Kalwaria in front of the image of Christ's Mother at the foot of the Cross.

The Pope understood this as a vital moment in his life of faith. He never doubted that Mary led him deeper into union with Christ. It was always clear to him that she could never lead anywhere else. Mary is the one who commands us to do whatever Jesus tells us.

What Karol came to be astonished by was the fact that Jesus entrusts His Mother to those who dedicate themselves to prayer. Why did Jesus entrust Mary to the Beloved Disciple? Spiritually, what does this mean for all those Christ loves and whom He has drawn to the mystery of the Cross in prayer? His encyclical *Mother of the Redeemer* includes an important explanation of this mystical reality in the context of Golgatha.

The Scriptures explain to us that Mary stood at the foot of the Cross with the Beloved Disciple. In this spiritual place, the threshold of saving access with God, in which the truth of our humanity and the truth of God's love coincide, a new kind of maternity was revealed to the world. This maternity is supernatural, a motherhood that is above the natural order. To reveal this, Jesus subordinates what is natural to the new supernatural reality that His saving work of redemption establishes. In the passage, Jesus seems to distance Himself from His Mother and to dispossess her when He says, "Woman, behold, your son!" (John 19:26).

Christ's words and actions concerning His Mother bear unique relation to her obedience to the Father. On the Cross, Christ dispossesses Himself of everything. He gives all that is most personal and dear to Him away out of love for the Father and for the sake of our salvation. His freedom, His dignity, His Mother, and His last breath are all offered for us as His sacrifice of praise.

From her fiat at the moment that He was conceived, to her radical following of Him to the Cross, she perseveres in pondering the truth of God in her heart. Even as her Son *seems* to reject her, she follows all the more closely. In fact, the true nature of her maternal relationship with the Lord emerges in this seeming rejection.

At the wedding feast at Cana, the Lord seems to reject her when He addresses her as "woman," but her reaction is like a queen mother whose request the king cannot reject (see John 2:3–5). Later, when someone exclaims that the womb that bore Him and the breasts that fed Him were blessed, the Word of the Father counters by declaring, rather, that those who hear His word and keep it are blessed (Luke 11:27–28). Again, when someone informs Him that His Mother and brothers are outside, the Son of God declares that only those who do the will of the Father are mother and brothers to Him. Then, he goes out to the mysterious woman (see Luke 8:19–21).

When He declares the blessedness of those who hear and believe Him, he subordinates natural bonds of human affection to the new supernatural bonds that faith in Him establishes. The new bonds we have by faith are greater than this life. This is why Christian faith gives us the freedom to renounce even our natural instinct for self-preservation. This means that by prayer we can subordinate our love for life to our love of God.

This Marian subordination of what is most naturally dear to us to what is supernatural and not familiar to us is a threshold into a deep truth about how we are to live. Cleaving to this life does not have to be our ultimate pursuit. Prayer rooted in devotion to our Lady opens us to that truth that even when we die, death is not the final word about our existence.

Mary, who stood beneath the Cross, is a sign to us that we have in us a love that is greater than death. A fire burns in our hearts that the deep waters of death cannot quench. Even as we are dispossessed of everything and everyone in death, Mary helps us follow Christ to the end. Mary, the Mother of Life Himself, helps to guide us and prays for us even at the solemn moment when we draw our last breath.

Mary is declared blessed not because of maternal instincts and biology, but because she believed, obeyed, and kept the Word spoken to her. She in fact conceived Him in her heart before she conceived Him in her womb. The Lord's mysterious way of relating with Mary reveals that the work of His new creation involves believing in His love and concern even when it is expressed in unfamiliar ways. By His grace, Jesus shows His power to re-create woman, making Mary the New Eve.

Each apparent rejection is actually an affirmation: the woman Mary, the New Eve, is the one who hears and keeps His word, and she is His Mother precisely because of her radical obedience of the will of the Father. Such is the power of the grace of Christ that it can reconstitute our humanity to conform to the truth He reveals. The sign of God's mysterious love that Mary provides throughout the ministry of Christ reaches its climax at the foot of the Cross. As at the wedding feast at Cana, Jesus, looking at His Mother, calls her "Woman." And then, He gives her to the disciple whom He loved. This Beloved Disciple likewise takes her into his home.[93]

---

[93] See John 19:26–27 and Blessed John Paul II, *Redemptoris Mater* 20–24.

Jesus' entrusting His Mother to the disciple whom He loves speaks to a very special grace offered to those who strive to begin to pray. When Jesus offered His beloved disciple the gift of His Mother, the beloved disciple took her into his home. This means he made the Lord's Mother part of his personal life, even his own life of prayer, his intimate devotion to Christ.

John Paul II was astounded at this gift. By dispossessing Himself of everything in this life, including His Mother, Jesus offers each of us His Mother and the gift of new life. If we choose to take Mary into our hearts, choose to welcome her into our lives, she offers us the same maternal affection she offered Jesus. It is a spiritual motherhood that Christ gives us through her. This spiritual maternity is as connected with our spiritual life as natural motherhood is with our natural life. Mary nurtures and protects us spiritually so that we can mature in our love for the Lord and in our devotion in prayer. By accepting the gift of Mary, we make ourselves, in a spiritual sense, her sons and daughters.

It is to this end that a tradition arose in the Catholic patrimony of prayer of consecrating oneself to Jesus through Mary. Sometimes called Marian Consecration, this spiritual act of welcoming Mary into one's life and entrusting her with everything allows her to entrust to that person everything in her maternal heart: the fruit of the most profound contemplation of her Son and the Work of redemption. Such an exchange of hearts between the Mother of the Lord and a disciple who welcomes her expands the life of prayer, so that our efforts to pray are infused with the prayers of the Virgin Mother.

Redeemed by the sacrifice of her Son on the Cross, Mary's natural motherhood has been transformed by His blood into a spiritual motherhood. She prays for every Christian that the gift of faith might be nurtured and come to maturity. She is able to lead those who welcome this maternal mediation of the grace of Christ into their hearts into the same obedient faith by which she followed her Son to the Cross to participate in His work of redemption.

Blessed Elizabeth of the Trinity understood this in a beautiful way. She reflects on the unique knowledge that Mary had of her Son, not only because she was His Mother, but more so because she accompanied her Son with faith from His conception all the way to His Crucifixion, pondering all these things in her heart.[94] Mary contemplated Jesus' obedience on the Cross more profoundly than any other human being.

This obedience, according to Blessed Elizabeth, was a great song of praise. Because Mary carries this song of praise in her heart, she can teach it to those who entrust themselves to her intercession.

Blessed Elizabeth of the Trinity describes this as His great canticle, a hymn of glory so beautiful and so hidden that no one knows it fully. Mary who was there, however, knows it deep enough to teach us this song of praise when we must pass through crucifying moments in our lives. Mary, who was with Christ and who was an intimate part of the Lord's final dispossession of everything for our sake, is able to teach us how to make our death into a beautiful canticle of praise too.

Because of this, in those painful crucifying moments of our lives, if we ask Mary, she will help us offer the same song of praise that Jesus offered on the Cross. She who magnifies the Lord also helps us magnify His glory and extend the work of redemption to the world. Through prayer guided by the Lord's gift of Mary's spiritual maternity, death becomes the making up in our own

---

[94] See Blessed Elizabeth of the Trinity, *Last Retreat*, nos. 40–41.

bodies "what is lacking in the suffering of Christ" (see Col. 1:24). Because Christ has given her to us, we have hope that, even through our dying bodies, we will at last render true "spiritual worship" (see John 4:23).

Throughout these pages on beginning to pray, I have tried to explain how in Christian contemplation the garden of our hearts is home to fire from above. Devotion to Mary is an important means of fostering this kind of prayer. Mary wants to teach the mystical wisdom that she learned at the foot of the Cross. Those who welcome Mary and allow her to teach them the heart of her Son come to know Mary as Elizabeth of the Trinity did. For Elizabeth and for all such disciples, Mary becomes for them *Janua Coeli*, the "Gate of Heaven."

Saint John Paul II lived out his intimacy with Christ Jesus by entrusting his life of prayer into the maternal hands of Mary. His motto, *Totus Tuus* (Wholly Yours), refers to this special relationship. She who obediently followed the Lord, who allowed herself to be raised in the order of grace from a natural motherhood to a supernatural motherhood, accompanies all those who allow themselves to be raised by her Son into the new existence of grace that Christian prayer makes possible. Those who will welcome Mary into their hearts will soon find themselves a vital part of the spiritual revolution initiated under John Paul II's leadership, a revolution that has already begun to change the world in which we live.

SPIRITUAL REVOLUTION AND
THE NEW EVANGELIZATION

"A revolution!" This is how Saint John Paul the Great under-stood the radical and widespread return to prayer being released in the world today. He sees this rediscovery of prayer as a vital contradiction. To pursue Christian holiness through prayer is to defy dehumanizing social forces that threaten to crush human dignity and freedom. This spiritual revolution is the beginning of a renewed effort to proclaim the gospel of Christ. The fruit of this return to Christian prayer is a New Evangelization.

At the beginning of his pontificate, in a small village just out-side Nowa Huta, he coined the phrase "new evangelization" dur-ing a homily. He was drawing a connection between the current pastoral landscape of the Church and the original evangelization inspired by the relic of the True Cross in the village. Then, as now, the Church carries out her mission in a non-Christian world.

Secular Nowa Huta was intentionally designed by the Com-munists without a parish. It was presumed that the modern worker, having gained control of his own destiny, no longer needed to waste time in prayer. When he was bishop of the area, Karol Wojtyla erected a cross with local workers. Every time it was taken down by Communist authorities, the future Pope and the people put it back up.

This expression of faith was more than an act of defiance in the face of the absolute claims of governmental power. It was more than the rejection of merely material values as the only determinate of human dignity. It was about prayer and the desire to have a community in which space for prayer, especially the Mass, was protected.

After he became Pope, Saint John Paul II knew from experience that God is more powerful than governments and cultural powers. He had already seen for himself that the faith was more profound than any political ideology or system. He was convinced that the world needs the living God and that Christians need to rediscover Christ in prayer. A world tormented by pessimism needs missionaries who have found hope in Christ. When he first spoke of a "new evangelization," it was a challenge to young people to set out on the path of holiness and become leaven within the Church and within society.

By World Youth Day '93, he was calling young people to lead the way in proclaiming the gospel of Christ. During this event, John Paul II's clarion call for a new evangelization went side by side with his call for a renewed interiority. He well understood that only spiritual maturity answers the needs of a culture exhausted in commercial and material pursuits. And, he insisted, the only path to spiritual maturity is through renewing our gaze on the face of Christ in prayer.

Until Saint John Paul II came to Denver in 1993 for World Youth Day, he did not have much reason to be confident that Americans would really respond to his call. Indeed, like most Europeans, he had only heard discouraging things about the Church in the United States. Even in America, in Denver itself, there was vehement skepticism that anything good could come from the religious event. In fact, everyone assumed the opposite.

In what was dubbed "the summer of violence," a terrible wave of gang violence swept through Denver in the weeks before World Youth Day.

In the middle of August, however, this narrative was turned upside down. The Pope, Denver, and the world experienced a moment of actual grace. With pilgrims coming from all over the world and the Holy Father's arrival, it was as if a whole new presence of Christ settled into the city.

The local response was one of beautiful hospitality. All over the city, one saw people at their very best. Even secular news commentators noted that Denver had dramatically changed, and on several occasions they too got caught up in the jubilation. Political leaders and law-enforcement officials were astounded to discover that, with the inflow of young people from around the world, both violent crime and petty theft actually decreased.

A prayerful sense of joyful solidarity permeated the Mile High City when John Paul II finally arrived. Even television news anchors were visible moved and noted the change. It was into this new social reality that the Pilgrim Pope gave an important word of hope, "Dear young people, I greet you in the name of Jesus Christ. He is the Way, the Truth ... *and the Life!*"

What followed may be one of the most prayerful gatherings in the history of the United States. Hundreds of thousands of young people from around the world walked, talked, sang, and prayed. They trod along Cherry Creek on a pilgrimage from lower downtown Denver all the way to Cherry Creek State Park for an all-night prayer vigil. Dehydration took its toll on many, and many emergency personnel went the extra mile to take care of these pilgrims. Even so, a spirit of joy and Christian mirth pervaded the whole event.

After making a private retreat high in the Rocky Mountains, the Holy Father joined the pilgrims in prayer during the vigil. Some of the pilgrims were overcome with exhaustion, but no one wanted to leave. There was a special bond between the youth and the Holy Father. The explanation for this is simple: true prayer deepens authentic solidarity. Indeed, the theme song for the event was "We Are One Body." The event ended with Mass on Sunday morning with faithful from all over the State of Colorado joining in.

At the heart of this gathering was a beautiful and profound encounter with the Lord. John Paul the Great asserted with great conviction that against all the seemingly insurmountable forces of death and in spite of the many false teachers of our times, Jesus Christ offers us our only true and realistic hope.

In fact, the young people did not want merely to muddle through life and to learn a new way to manage life's pain. They had come together because they believed this Pope was offering them something more meaningful. The Pope also encouraged the young people of the world not to fear a life-changing encounter with Christ.

Jesus, he insisted, was the only answer to the deepest needs of the human heart. This is why so many felt their hearts moved to prayer when he reproposed Jesus' words in John 10:10, "I came that they may have life, and have it abundantly."

The encounter culminated in action. Genuine prayer always leads to a converted life, a life lived for love. This is why the Pope also challenged all the pilgrims to proclaim the gospel boldly "from the rooftops" of the modern metropolis. By our dedication to a close relationship with Christ in prayer, the Pope insisted that we could build a culture of life and civilization of love, repeating, "Be proud of the gospel of Christ!"

Many participants, even non-Christians, left with the desire to enter more deeply into prayer, to seek the living God. As for the Pope, he came to see this as a great grace, a history-changing moment. This is saying a lot for a world leader who helped bring about the fall of Communism in Europe. It meant the beginning of something new for the whole world, something astonishing that the world did not expect. For years afterward, when Denver was mentioned to him, Saint John Paul II would exclaim, "Revolution!"

A spiritual revival began to take hold. It was as if new life returned to a patient whom many had already given up for dead, and this new life was contagious. Nationally, Catholic media, such as the Eternal Word Television Network, were injected with a renewed sense of vigor and purpose. Young people began to look at the priesthood and religious life in a new way. Movements such as Christ in the City gained new momentum. The religious sensibility of America had been touched.

John Paul II's Mystical Wisdom

If we want to continue the spiritual revolution, we need to acquire the mystical wisdom that the Pilgrim Pope witnessed to. Saint John Paul would dedicate the first hours of every morning to Mass and silent prayer. He prayed ardently and with great confidence in the face of situations that seemed humanly impossible to solve. His being a catalyst for helping to change political realities was possible only because of his intense prayer life. He prayed from the depths of his heart with great intensity. He sighed, he groaned, he wept. Sometimes, his whole body would shake. His prayers were ardent.

What was the secret of Saint John Paul's prayer? We can only guess that it had to do with the suffering and difficulties he confronted in his personal life. By the time he was twenty-one years of age, he had lost all his siblings and his parents. Nazi Germany invaded from the West and Communist Russia from the East. Many of his closest friends, including many of his Jewish friends from school, were imprisoned and executed. Against overwhelming military and political powers, he joined the struggle to protect his people, his language, and his culture even before his decision to become a priest. In this, his life of prayer was being forged to confront evil and not allow it to go unanswered.

More than the military and cultural struggles that he faced, his prayer grew through the wonderful connections and friendships that he discovered through his confrontation with evil. As a seminarian, he connected with the laborers in the stone quarry where the Nazis forced them to labor. As a priest, he connected with young people and students organizing camping trips and theater performances.

Having guided his flock during Communism's intense push to secularize his society, as the archbishop of Krakow, he knew people needed God to protect what was most precious and important in their lives. This is why, when the Communists would not allow workers to have a parish church, Karol Wojtyla chose to stand with them, to celebrate Mass with them and to raise the Cross of Christ with them. When he became Pope he already understood the fear and lack of confidence that had gripped the Church. Into this he spoke a word of truth that we need to hear again today when he confidently preached, "Do not be afraid to open wide the doors to Christ."

Open the Doors to Christ Anew

If we are asking, at least interiorly, whether our patrimony of prayer is still relevant, whether any of it is real, then it is long past time for us to reconsider what Saint John Paul II proposed throughout his ministry. Like him, our prayer can grow if we will take it into the difficult social realities of our day. In solidarity with John Paul II's devotion to Christ, we will discover that God is guiding us through it all.

If he had to confront dehumanizing ideologies with his prayer, we also must confront the violence, despondency, and grave scandal that have marked our time with so much confusion and discouragement. We have not really confronted the near-total genocide of Christian populations in Islamic countries, the epidemic of young men driven by either rage or despondency to destroy themselves and everyone around them, the failure to protect the innocence of our children, the insane acceptance of drugs as an appropriate form of recreation, the explosion of Internet pornography, the widespread denial about the realities of sex trafficking and slavery in our communities, and the horrific scandals followed by even more horrific scandals involving those in pastoral places of trust. In all of this, the most vulnerable are at risk because not many have the heart to confront the overwhelming evil these social developments present. The life of prayer lived by Saint John Paul invites us to do better than this.

In particular today, we are witnessing the complete social destruction of the sacred institution of marriage and family. Long undermined by widespread divorce, contraception, and abortion, the friendship love of husband and wife is crushed under the failure to offer clear teaching on its dignity and greatness and the even greater failure to live these teachings out. Without this most vital form of connection, all other kinds of connection that bind a society together are at complete and total risk.

If we follow the footsteps of the Pilgrim Pope, we know that by a renewed life of prayer, the love of God can raise up marriage and family again. By learning to pray as John Paul II did in the midst of our struggles, what is evil in our social reality today will not be the last word about who we are as a people or as individuals. Here, in the conclusion of these reflections on prayer, we discover that this kind of devotion is stronger than death. This connection with one another by a love that cannot be defeated is given to us by Christ through the gift of His Mother in the spiritual life.

Mystical Wisdom in the Face of Death

In the days before his death, sick and weak as he was, Saint John Paul II pulled himself up to his window and peeked out at the crowds of young people who were praying for him in Saint Peter's Square. The presence of young people always gave him new strength. They were drawn to him. What drew them was not great skills of oratory or the promise that they would be entertained. Instead, the love of God that dwelt in him through prayer was calling out to them.

He had reached out to them in love because his prayer compelled him to. Now they were drawn to him and wanted to be connected with him because of what they witnessed as the fruit of his prayer. It was a solidarity of prayer and love. After recalling his many visits to young people around the world, he thanked them for coming to pray for him, "I have sought you out and now you come to me.... Thank you."

His words were from the heart. The presence of the young people and other pilgrims, their witness together in prayer, was a great consolation to him. In the face of all kinds of evil over which he could not help but be concerned, they were a great sign the Lord had heard his prayer. They shared together a solidarity in the Lord because they, with him, were not afraid to open wide the doors to Christ.

Our Spiritual Home

As his last days approached, Blessed John Paul II expressed his desire to go to the Father's house. In his heart, he already knew that the Father's house was his true home. Home is a place of communion and friendship. It is permeated with the peace and joy that is found only in loving those entrusted to us, and even more in knowing that we are loved. In this life and in this world, we are never really at home. We are never fully at peace. Our joy is never quite what it ought to be. Deep inside we know we are made for another kind of existence.

Our heavenly homeland, the spiritual household to which we belong, is the bosom of the Trinity. The fire of God's love warms and enlightens all that is good, beautiful, and true about our humanity. It purifies us of all that is banal, compromising, and mediocre. It sets us afire — not a fire that destroys noble aspirations, deepest hope, and beautiful desires, but the holy fire that set ablaze but did not destroy the burning bush that Moses saw. This fire makes the ground holy and draws men and women to its astonishing glory. As we draw ever closer to the heart of the Trinity, we become more fully human because the humanity of Christ on fire with the love of the Father is our pathway. It is in this living flame that our humanity is finally at home.

This paradox reveals the beautiful mystery of our life in Christ: the more connected we are with Him, the more He connects us together with everything that most matters. We are in his image. If He is the gift given to us from above, we are most fully ourselves, the more we dispossess ourselves of what is here below and live for what is above.

This is true freedom from the absolute claims that the powers and principalities of this life make on us. We are more than cogs in a wheel, and God's project in us is greater than any cultural or social project in this world. In this web of grace, we discover the truth about our humanity by giving ourselves in love for one another as He did for us. In this world, such freedom of spirit is fire from on high.

The living flame that moves us to dispossess ourselves of our self in prayer enables us to give ourselves in love even more. The more completely we conform our lives to Christ crucified by offering our earthly existence to God, the more unique and unrepeatable a gift to the world we become.

This gift of self on fire with the Holy Spirit makes possible all kinds of love that the world does not know but desperately longs for. In this fire of freedom, there is a living communion in which all that is most noble and good about humanity can thrive. The Father's house, where this fire burns and into which Jesus invites us, is everlasting fellowship. This life ablaze with love and truth awaits us not only at the end of our days, but right now, in this present moment, a moment that Blessed Elizabeth of the Trinity explains is "eternity begun and still in progress."[95]

The Fire of Prayer

We have shared together some of the insights that are firing up a whole new generation of young men ready to climb the Lord's mountain and eager to enter the garden of His love. They want to serve the Bridegroom for whose coming they yearn. They are neither enchanted by the empty promises of pop culture nor afraid of the heartless brutality it incubates. They see God's love, not moral failure, as the defining characteristic of humanity. Captivated by the One whom they have set out to find, they are dedicated to helping the world welcome Him with joy.

[95] Blessed Elizabeth of the Trinity, *Heaven in Faith*, no. 1.

Although not all of these have been ordained, the decision to do something beautiful for God binds them together in friendship. Often misunderstood, even by those close to them, they have given up everything to serve their Crucified Master. Enduring daily trials, hardships, and challenges, they have found an unshakable foundation in the Risen Lord through prayer. Their effectiveness, faithfulness, and fruitfulness are testimony to the power of Christ Jesus and the spiritual revolution started under the leadership of John Paul II.

If your heart is drawn to the hidden mountain and secret garden, now is the time; this is the hour. Do not delay. Do not be afraid. As Blessed John Paul II exhorted us, "Be proud of the Gospel of Christ. Shout it from the rooftops!"

A spiritual revolution has begun, and the Lord Himself is inviting you to make this journey and to join His cause. The blessings He has predestined you to share are indispensable in the divine calling we share together during the brief span of our earthly lives: the vocation to build a culture of life and a civilization of love, a place in which the genuinely human will thrive—where the glory of God is man fully alive.[96]

---

[96] Saint Irenaeus, *Against Heresies* 4:20:7.

ANTHONY LILLES

A Catholic theologian and the married father of three young-adult children, Dr. Anthony Lilles serves in the Archdiocese of Los Angeles as academic dean of Saint John's Seminary in Camarillo and as academic adviser for Juan Diego House of Priestly Formation for Seminarians. He is a graduate of Franciscan University in Steubenville and holds a doctorate from the Angelicum in Rome, and his research and personal life are formed by the spiritual doctrine of the Carmelite Doctors of the Church and Blessed Elizabeth of the Trinity. With Dan Burke of EWTN, he helped to found the Avila Institute of Spiritual Formation, which provides online courses to students around the world.

SPIRITUAL DIRECTION
SERIES

SOPHIA INSTITUTE PRESS

If this book has caused a stir in your heart to continue to pursue your relationship with God, we invite you to explore two extraordinary resources, SpiritualDirection.com and the Avila Institute for Spiritual Formation.

The readers of SpiritualDirection.com reside in almost every country of the world where hearts yearn for God. It is the world's most popular English site dedicated to authentic Catholic spirituality.

The Students of the Avila Institute for Spiritual Formation sit at the feet of the rich and deep well of the wisdom of the saints.

You can find more about the Avila Institute at
WWW.AVILA-INSTITUTE.COM.

SOPHIA
INSTITUTE PRESS

Sophia Institute is a nonprofit institution that seeks to nurture the spiritual, moral, and cultural life of souls and to spread the Gospel of Christ in conformity with the authentic teachings of the Roman Catholic Church.

Sophia Institute Press fulfills this mission by offering translations, reprints, and new publications that afford readers a rich source of the enduring wisdom of mankind.

Sophia Institute also operates two popular online Catholic resources: CrisisMagazine.com and CatholicExchange.com.

Crisis Magazine provides insightful cultural analysis that arms readers with the arguments necessary for navigating the ideological and theological minefields of the day. *Catholic Exchange* provides world news from a Catholic perspective as well as daily devotionals and articles that will help you to grow in holiness and live a life consistent with the teachings of the Church.

In 2013, Sophia Institute launched Sophia Institute for Teachers to renew and rebuild Catholic culture through service to Catholic education. With the goal of nurturing the spiritual, moral, and cultural life of souls, and an abiding respect for the role and work of teachers, we strive to provide materials and programs that are at once enlightening to the mind and ennobling to the heart; faithful and complete, as well as useful and practical.

Sophia Institute gratefully recognizes the Solidarity Association for preserving and encouraging the growth of our apostolate over the course of many years. Without their generous and timely support, this book would not be in your hands.

www.SophiaInstitute.com
www.CatholicExchange.com
www.CrisisMagazine.com
www.SophiaInstituteforTeachers.org

Sophia Institute Press® is a registered trademark of Sophia Institute. Sophia Institute is a tax-exempt institution as defined by the Internal Revenue Code, Section 501(c)(3). Tax I.D. 22-2548708.